WHEN GOD COMES DOWN

Daniel Sloan, PhD

IHP Academia

Copyright © 2025 Daniel Sloan. All rights reserved. Except for brief quotations in critical publications or reviews, no part of this book may be reproduced in any manner without prior written permission from the publisher: admin@illativehousepress.com.

IHP Academia
An Imprint of Illative House Press, LLC
500 E. Elm St.
West Frankfort, IL 62896
IllativeHousePress.com

All IHP publications are available through Amazon.com.

Paperback ISBN: 979-8-9990929-2-2
Hardcover ISBN: 979-8-9990929-3-9

Cover artwork: Frode Inge Helland, CC BY-SA 3.0 <https://creativecommons.org/licenses/by-sa/3.0>, via Wikimedia Commons
Cover design: Illative House Press

Praise for *When God Comes Down*

Having had the privilege of working alongside the author under Dr. Hindson, I can confidently say that Daniel Sloan has beautifully captured the heart of his mentor in this book. *When God Comes Down* challenges its readers to trust in the intricate workings of God's will, drawing from His past examples of intervention to strengthen our hope for the future. It is truly encouraging to see Dr. Hindson's mantle being picked up by the next generation of biblical scholars, carrying forward his legacy with faithfulness.

    John Roselle, Senior Pastor of Plainedge Church in Bethpage, NY

God is at work making all things new, and in these pages, Sloan provides ten concrete biblical examples of God's intervention in human history. With a scholarly overview that moves from creation to new-creation, Sloan's work honors both his mentor, Dr. Ed Hindson, and our incomparable God. This work is simultaneously theological and practical, and it serves to remind everyone of God's love, provision, presence, patience, salvation, and ultimate triumph!

    Dr. Charles Joshua Parrott, Vice President for Christian Life and Service and University Chaplain, Gardner-Webb University

In my 30 years of pastoral ministry, I have encountered multiple individuals who have wondered aloud, "Where is God?" "Where is God in my struggle? Where is God in my pain? Where is God in my circumstance?" In essence, they are asking, "Does God intervene when I need Him? *When God Comes Down* offers a thorough exploration of God's intervention throughout history, as detailed in the Bible. Dr. Daniel Sloan dives deeply into significant Biblical events, addressing questions about God's timing and choices regarding His intervention in human affairs, culminating in an uplifting message of trust in God's overarching plan. This is a great read for small group studies or is an excellent resource for personal reflection regarding God's involvement in our lives.

    Rob Rosenbalm, Pastor, Fairfield West Baptist Church in Fairfield, Ohio

When God Comes Down by Dr. Daniel Sloan is a thoughtful and theologically rich exploration of God's presence in human history. Bridging biblical narrative with contemporary relevance, Sloan skillfully weaves scriptural exposition with personal and modern illustrations, making complex theological themes accessible and applicable. The book is grounded in solid scholarship and supported by extensive biblical content, making it a valuable resource for both ministry practitioners and academic settings. I highly recommend this work as supplemental reading for courses in biblical theology, pastoral studies, or spiritual formation. It also serves as an excellent tool for church leaders seeking to deepen their understanding of divine engagement in the human story.

>Dr. Rob Van Engen, Associate Professor, Liberty University John W. Rawlings School of Divinity

In *When God Comes Down*, Dr. Daniel Sloan leads readers through evidence of how God makes His presence felt in all circumstances in the Bible. Each chapter considers a moment in Scripture when God worked for His people by being present and active in their lives, with careful attention given to personal application. All people would benefit from reading this book to learn how God showed up in the Bible and how He wants to show up in our lives today.

>Matthew Watson, Pastor at Mt. Pisgah Baptist Church in Ewing, Kentucky

Contents

Introduction The Origin of This Book	6
Chapter One Garden of Eden: Provision	8
Chapter Two Tower of Babel: Judgment	21
Chapter Three The Exodus: Deliverance	30
Chapter Four Mount Carmel: Power	42
Chapter Five Hezekiah: Healing	54
Chapter Six The Assyrian Invasion: Incomparability	63
Chapter Seven Bethlehem: Person	75
Chapter Eight Golgotha: Atonement	85
Chapter Nine Pentecost: Permanence	94
Chapter Ten Armageddon: Triumph	105
Conclusion Why Does God Pick and Choose When to Come Down?	115
Bibliography	117
Endnotes	120

Introduction

The Origin of This Book

The idea of this book was born about eight years ago. My mentor, Dr. Ed Hindson, a world-renowned speaker and theologian, was the Dean of the School of Divinity at Liberty University. He also served as the teacher on *The King is Coming* telecast from World Prophetic Ministries. Because of these two roles, people asked Doc to speak at various churches and conferences around the United States and occasionally internationally. He would travel 2-3 weekends a month to talk all over the country, even well into his seventies.

As Doc traveled throughout the country and spoke to various people throughout the local church, one of the questions that kept coming up was, "Where is God?" or "Why is God not intervening in either my life or in the nation?" After hearing this question at least a dozen times, Doc devised a sermon entitled "When God Comes Down." He based this sermon on Isaiah 64:1: "Oh, that You would rend the heavens! That You would come down! That the mountains might shake at Your presence—." In the sermon, Doc talked about how it is natural for humanity to want God to come down and intervene in our lives, just as the Jews cried out in the Book of Isaiah.

Doc preached the sermon several times at various churches and got a good response. However, he wasn't thrilled with the sermon outline he had developed. During this time, I was privileged to serve as Doc's Teaching Assistant while completing my PhD. We went out to lunch one day after he returned from speaking and talked about his sermon. He decided that he would keep Isaiah 64:1 as the opening salvo of the sermon but that he needed to give concrete examples throughout the Bible of different times and ways that God came down and intervened throughout human history. Doc, similarly to God, liked to have seven points, and so that lunch, we created a seven-point outline of the various times and ways that God came down throughout the Bible.

Doc preached this revised sermon probably a half dozen times or so at various churches and found that it resonated with people, to the point that he asked me if I would be a part of expanding the sermon into book form. We also added three more additions to the examples of God coming down, giving us ten examples to work through. We planned to work on this book as soon as we finished the *Evangelical Study Bible*, in which Doc served as the general editor, and I served as the managing editor. Unfortunately, just as we finished that project in the summer of 2022, Doc went home to be with the Lord. It is a great honor to finish this project and honor Doc's legacy.

The Premise of When God Comes Down

When bad things happen, people ask, "Why doesn't God do something about…" or "Why doesn't God come down and fix this?". I remember when September 11th, 2001 happened. I was just eleven years old, in the sixth grade, on that day. That morning, we were right in the middle of art class when my teacher, Mr. Brown, suddenly came back into the classroom. This action differed from a usual day because he usually left the classroom while the art teacher did her thing. He pulled her aside, whispered something in her ear, and she turned pale white. He then rolled over the television in the back of the room and put it in the front of the classroom. He explained the situation to our class and then turned on the television for the news. Being in Ohio, most of us had never even heard of the World Trade Center, but the magnitude of the situation was not lost on any of us as we watched the news that morning.

Over the next few days, you may remember how crazy of a time that was in our nation. While there was a considerable return to churches, at least for a few weeks, many wondered how God could have allowed this to happen. Why would God have allowed these terrorists to kill thousands of innocent people? Why did God not come down and stop them in some way? Some even began to question why God allowed terrible things to happen. If God is a loving God, why does He not come down and intervene in our lives all the time and stop every bad thing from happening?

The truth is that God has been coming down and intervening throughout human history since the very beginning. This book will look at ten different times when God did come down/will come down and interact with humanity. Each chapter picks a specific element of how God interacted with humanity and will focus on the passage in question while also pulling out applications from the stories of the biblical characters and applications that cross over to a contemporary audience. The book's goal is to show that God has come down throughout history to help His people and will continue to come down through the Second Coming, culminating in God's relationship with humanity being restored permanently, with Jesus reigning and ruling the entire earth. Join me as we begin seeing what happens when God comes down!

Chapter One

Garden of Eden: Provision

Adam, where are you? Genesis 3:9

Imagine one day sitting in a beautiful restaurant served by one of the best chefs in the world. You have just finished a fabulous meal when the chef comes out and offers you a choice of desserts. If you are like me, you like to see and smell your desserts before you order, so the chef wheels out dozens of desserts on various carts out to your table. You have cheesecake, chocolate cake, cookies, pies, puddings, pastries, and every type of dessert you could imagine. Hungry yet?

However, then the chef makes a bizarre request. He points out the apple crumb streusel pie and tells you that you can pick out any dessert, but you cannot have the apple crumb streusel pie. Some people might go, "Okay, that's fine," and move on. Most of us would immediately go right to the apple streusel pie. We would look at it. We could smell it. What is up with this pie? Why can't I have this pie? What makes this pie so unique? Dozens of other desserts are available, but we would immediately check out the one dessert we cannot have. That is where we find ourselves in Genesis 3.

Perhaps no chapters of the Bible are as familiar to believers and non-believers alike as the first three chapters of Genesis. Reading the creation story of Genesis 1-2 has occurred for generations, and most people know of the Fall of Adam and Eve. However, the events immediately after the Fall are much more obscure. They are not as widely recognized as the previous chapters because people tend to stop reading the story. It is through these events that God comes down and provides both short-term and long-term provision for humanity immediately after the sinful events of the Fall.

Immediate Context

Opening the pages of Genesis three occurs directly after the creation events of Genesis 1-2. The universe has been created and ordered. God established the Earth with all of its living creatures. Finally, God established Adam and Eve as the first humans; Adam and Eve were married by God at their creation and placed in the Garden of Eden, a paradise established by God for their work and enjoyment. God gave them only one restriction: "Of every tree of the garden you may freely eat; but of the tree of the knowledge of good and evil you shall not eat, for in the day that you eat of it you shall surely die." (2:16-17). The chapter ends with them married and living in the Garden, completely naked and unashamed.

The Tempter (3:1)

The amount of time between chapters two and three is unknown, as the author did not provide any temporal markings.[1] However, it does appear to be a relatively short time because Adam and Eve do not have children until after the Fall. Whether this was a few weeks, months, or even years is simply impossible to know. The author of Genesis only gives two-timing elements in the story at this point. Adam would live to be 930 years old and have Seth at 130 years old.[2] Thus, 130 years passed from Adam's creation to Seth's birth at the end of chapter four, giving the timeline a lot of wiggle room.

Verse one begins the story by introducing a new character, the serpent. The identity of this serpent is one of the major interpretive challenges of the passage. Traditionally, the serpent has been viewed throughout Christian history as Satan, either possessing a physical animal or having some physical form. The New Testament defends this, identifying the serpent as Satan in Romans 16:20, Revelation 12:9, and Revelation 20:2. This would also explain how the serpent was able to communicate with Eve in the passage.

However, some Old Testament scholars, while not denying that Satan was ultimately behind the serpent based on the New Testament, argue that the original audience of Genesis would have had no way to recognize that the serpent was Satan or even know that Satan existed at all at that time. For example, John Walton writes,

> It is important to recognize that the serpent is simply classified as one of the wild animals. This classification mitigates any speculation concerning an Israelite understanding of a hidden identity of the serpent. There is no god or demon or genie lurking beneath the guise of the serpent. It comes with nothing out of the ordinary that would alert the woman's suspicions. Of course, we cannot help but wonder what she thought when the serpent talked... There is no hint in the Old Testament that the serpent of Genesis 2–3 was either identified as Satan or was thought to be inspired by Satan.[3]

Similarly, Mangum writes,

> There has been much scholarly debate over the serpent's identity in Gen 3:1. Scholars such as Calvin and Mathews traditionally interpret it as the devil or an animal used by the devil. However, as Sarna and others note, this interpretation is not in the Old Testament and does not appear until the Jewish Apocryphal book Wisdom of Solomon, which dates to the first century. The writings of New Testament authors, including Paul (Rom 16:20) and John (Rev 12:9), also reflect

this understanding. Cassuto and others argue that such an interpretation introduces concepts into the Genesis text that the ancient audience would not have recognized.[4]

While it may be impossible to clearly understand who Eve thought the serpent was at the time or what the original audience would have thought, a canonical reading clearly asserts that the serpent was Satan. Mathews sums it up nicely, writing, "The snake is more than a literal snake; rather, it is Satan's presence in the garden."[5]

While the passage may not be clear about the serpent's identity, it gives several additional attributes. First, the text says the serpent "was more cunning than any beast of the field." This attribute prepares the reader to understand that the serpent probably should not be trusted. The Hebrew word for cunning, sometimes translated in English as crafty, עָרוּם has a bit of ambiguity to it about being a positive trait or a negative trait. Job 15:5 negatively uses the term in the vein of iniquity. It is used similarly in Job 5:12-13 and Exodus 21:14. However, David is called עָרוּם by Saul in 1 Samuel 23:22 because he was able to escape Saul's traps. Thus, the term itself does not necessarily bring a negative connotation but shows something unique about the serpent.

Second, the text says that the Lord God had made the serpent. While the original context of Genesis would assume this as there would be no other option based on Genesis 1-2, once later revelation clarified that this serpent was indeed Satan, the statement is critical in eliminating any form of dualism. Mathews writes, "This dismisses any notion of a competing dualism since the animal owes its existence to God."[6] Satan, while incredibly strong and dangerous, is not equal to God in nature or power and was indeed created by God at some point in history. While Genesis does not describe the Fall of Satan in any detail or even explain where he came from, he is not an equal to God.

The verse ends with the first lie recorded in the Scriptures. The serpent, talking to Eve, questions God's limitations on humanity. He asks, "Has God indeed said, 'You shall not eat of every tree of the garden'?" This questioning is a lie and a misrepresentation of the commands of God. God had told humanity to avoid the one tree of the knowledge of good and evil. Satan instead makes it seem that God is being unfair and even harsh in his limitations, denying humanity access to any of the trees in the garden. In essence, he is arguing that God is a tyrant, unwilling to allow humanity any access to the beauty and resources that they see every day.

Humanity's Failing (3:2-7)

At first, Eve gives what appears to be a strong response to Satan's question, with one caveat. She responds, "And the woman said to the serpent, "We may eat the fruit of the trees of the garden; but of the fruit of the tree which is in the midst of the garden, God has said, 'You shall not eat it, nor shall you touch it, lest you die" (3:2-3). Eve was correct in rejecting Satan's assertion that God had told them not to eat from any of the trees but only one specific tree. However, she added that the condition that God commanded was that they should not touch it. As the text states, God had never told Adam and Eve not to touch the tree but to not eat from it. It is not clear where Eve came up with this restriction. Perhaps they had misunderstood God's command. It is more likely that Adam had told Eve not to touch it as a safeguard.[7] Regardless of where it came from, it was an embellishment of legalism that God had not stated and that Satan would use to demean the character of God.   Satan's response shows his cunningness in the passage. He immediately jumped on the idea of death that Eve had mentioned, countering with a promise that she would not die. However, he does so in a very clever way. Walton explains, "The serpent's statement can therefore be paraphrased something like, "Don't think that death is such an immediate threat." The link to the next statement creates the sense that, according to the serpent, it was never really God's intention to put them to death. "He only said that to discourage you from acquiring the marvelous properties of the tree." In effect, the serpent does not actually contradict God; he only suggests that there is nothing to worry about."[8] Maybe Eve did not pick up on this subtle nuance, but it is clear that it, at the very least, prevented her from fearing the immediate consequences of her future sin. Satan had convinced her that eating the fruit would not lead directly to her death, maybe just the possibility of death in the future.

    Why, then, would Eve even attempt something that would even bring about a possibility of death? Because of the false promise of Satan found in verse five, "For God knows that in the day you eat of it your eyes will be opened, and you will be like God, knowing good and evil." While the words themselves are valid in many ways in that Adam and Eve will "know good and evil," as seen in verse twenty-two, Satan deceives Eve. He attacks the character of God. He makes it seem like God is holding something good back from humanity. If Adam and Eve partake in the action, they will become just like God. Technically, God was holding something back from humanity, but it was not good but sin and death. He wasn't doing something to limit humanity but to protect it. Mangum says it well when he states, "By saying this, the serpent casts doubt on God's motivation, making it appear that God issued the prohibition to protect His position rather than humanity's innocence."[9] He downplays the idea of knowing good and evil, making it sound like humanity should want to know. However, the only way for that to occur is to usher in sin into the world. Thus, Satan, as he so often does, uses deception to both downplay the consequences of sin while also overpromising on its rewards. Sin would never make humanity like God; it would instead drive humanity away from God's presence.

While Satan had opened the door of temptation, he could not force humanity to walk through it. Eve still had to take that opportunity for three reasons: the tree was good for food, pleasant to the eyes, and desirable to make one wise (3:6). 1 John 2:16 describes these three as "the lust of the flesh, the lust of the eyes, and the pride of life." It looked good and, based upon Satan's deception, would lead to a false promise of being like God. Eve believed that God was holding them back from something tremendous and, therefore, went against the warnings and limitations of God. She then eats the fruit in direct disobedience to the commands of God.

The question in many readers' minds is this: where is Adam? The end of verse six answers the question: "She also gave to her husband with her, and he ate." Does this mean that Adam was standing next to her the whole time when Satan was deceiving her, and he did not intervene, or does the text allow for a vaguer interpretation, possibly that he only showed up after she had eaten the fruit? Walton argues that "Adam was there with Eve. What else can verse 6 mean besides that he was present at the temptation?"[10] Similarly, Mathews writes, "Although 'with her' does not in itself demand that he is present since the serpent speaks 'to the woman,' nevertheless, the action of the verse implies that Adam is a witness to the dialogue. 'You' at each place in 3:1–5 is plural and thus suggests his presence. However, there is no indication that he too is deceived by the serpent."[11] Hence, it seems clear in the text that Adam was at least present in some capacity for the event, either standing near Eve or in the vicinity to be aware of what was happening in some capacity.

The sin of Adam was then twofold. First, he failed to protect his wife adequately. If he was present as the text leads, he should have immediately rebuked the serpent when the serpent started to question God's character and integrity. Second, and perhaps even more damaging, Adam did this willingly, according to the text of Genesis and other biblical texts. Indeed, 2 Corinthians 11:3 and 1 Timothy 2:14 acknowledge that the serpent deceived Eve. However, 1 Timothy 2:14 also states, "And Adam was not deceived". This lack of deception has to do with Adam being the one who received the prohibition before Eve's creation or that Adam should have known that the serpent was evil based upon his blasphemies of God.

There are few verses in Scripture gloomier than the first half of verse seven. The text states, "Then the eyes of both of them were opened, and they knew that they were naked." This observation of nakedness is connected back to earlier statements made in 3:5 and 2:25. In 3:5, Satan had promised eating the fruit would open Eve's eyes. However, his deception had made that seem like a positive characteristic. In contrast, Eve now knew what sin was and that she and Adam had partaken in that sin. Wenham states it well when he says, "The snake's prediction is literally fulfilled, but their vision is somewhat of a letdown."[12] Prior to eating the fruit, they were naively innocent. Now, they have greater knowledge but have lost their innocence. Before, they did not know the impact of sin; now, they know what sin is firsthand.

The first experiential impact of their sin was the knowledge that they were naked, both physically and spiritually. Before, in 2:25, they had been naked and yet felt no shame or guilt. Now, they immediately felt those emotions come into their conscience. Something that God had made perfect, their nakedness in the garden, had now been corrupted with the Fall. Their immediate response should have been to cry out to God in repentance. Instead, it was to try to cover up their shameful nakedness with fig leaves. While the fig leaves could temporarily cover their physical nakedness, albeit in a very partial and temporary manner, it could do nothing with the spiritual nakedness that had now befallen them.

The Confrontation (3:8-13)

At this moment in history, God came down for the first time to interact with humanity and eventually offer divine intervention. First, however, God had to find and confront humanity's new situation. The text states, "And they heard the sound of the LORD God walking in the garden in the cool of the day" (3:8a). God had come down from Heaven and had come to visit with His creation, both nature and humanity. It is unknown if this was something that God regularly did or if this was a unique situation. Walton notes, "We are not told that this was a regular occurrence, but neither does the text indicate that it was unusual."[13] However, the idea of "walking with God" is found throughout the Old Testament as a sign of being in the right relationship with Him. Two chapters later, in 5:22, it is stated that Enoch walked with God. In 6:9, Noah walked with God. In 17:1, Abraham is commanded to walk before God. In 48:15, Abraham and Isaac walked with God.

Adam and Eve, instead of walking with God in faithfulness, now hide themselves in sinful shame. Their efforts to cover their shame have failed. While they could temporarily cover their physical nakedness, they knew that they could do nothing about their spiritual nakedness. Instead of meeting with God and asking for forgiveness and deliverance, they attempt to hide from Him in the garden that He had created. They failed to realize that it is impossible to hide from the Creator of the universe. God already knew what had happened and exactly where and why they were hiding.

However, God, like a loving parent, wanted Adam and Eve to come out and admit their sinful actions. He already knew the answers to all the questions He would pose but wanted them to explain both what and why the Fall had occurred. Verse nine begins a series of four questions from God to man. First, He asks, "Where are you?" It wasn't so much the location that God was interested in, but why did Adam and Eve need to hide from Him? Regardless of whether this was a regular occurrence of God coming down to see them or not, it was clear that their unwillingness to meet with Him was a dramatic change in their relationship. Interestingly, God called out to Adam specifically and not to Eve or to both of them. He is trying to get Adam to explain his sin because he was the leader of the family unit. God told him not to eat the fruit, but he failed to stop it from happening.

Adam's response to God is less than ideal. First, he acknowledged that he had heard God's presence. Therefore, it was not simply a misunderstanding. God had not snuck up on them, but they had instead known He was coming. Then Adam let the cat out of the bag with two statements. He acknowledged he was afraid because of his nakedness. Both concepts, fear and nakedness, should not have been possible in a pre-fallen world. He then admitted that he had tried to hide from Him instead of coming to God in repentance for his actions. Adam was taking very little, if any, responsibility for his sin. This lack of taking responsibility will only get worse as the conversation continues.

God responds with two more questions. First, He asks Adam who told him that he was naked. The last time God interacted with Adam at the end of chapter two, Adam had been naked and unashamed. Something had changed that had caused him to be ashamed of his nakedness. Ironically, when God asked who told him that he was naked, the response was reflective as Adam and Eve themselves had recognized their nakedness instead of having to be told by another being like the serpent. Their sinful nature had ratted them out.

Second, God then asked Adam if he had eaten from the tree. God already knew the answer to the question, both when the event happened and based on Adam's response. However, He hopes that with this response, Adam will take the blame and repent of his disobedience. He is like a parent coming home to a broken lamp and a baseball, still asking what happened to the children even though it is completely obvious based on the circumstances. He wants Adam to acknowledge his sin rather than blame someone else.

If God wanted Adam to take responsibility, then he did the complete opposite by blaming both Eve and God. He blames Eve for giving him the fruit, even though it is apparent in the text that he knew exactly where the fruit came from and the potential consequences of eating it. Adam had not accidentally eaten something based on lousy knowledge from Eve; Adam had blatantly eaten the fruit. He even pulled God into his blame game, saying that it was the woman God gave him. Essentially, he says, "God, if you had not given me this woman as a wife, then I would never have eaten that fruit." Thus, Adam took zero responsibility for his actions.

This section ends with God moving on to question Eve. If Adam had not accepted responsibility for the sinful action, maybe Eve would. Instead, she follows in her husband's footsteps and blames the serpent, saying that the serpent deceived her. Her response is at least a little more accurate than Adam's, as the serpent deceived her, but she still takes no blame for the action. Thus, humanity's response to the confrontation is blaming each other or the devil.

The Consequences (3:14, 16-19)

God begins giving out His consequences first with the serpent in verse fourteen. Mathews sums up the punishment well when he states

> These punishments relate to the snake's life of humiliation and subjugation in the natural world. God's condemnation is not directed against the reptile per se but against the adversary that it represents. While some Jewish interpreters surmised that the serpent must have originally been four-legged, there is no compelling reason for this conclusion. It is enough to describe the present characteristics of the snake, which indicate by themselves the disgrace of the beast.[14]

Thus, God first humbles the snake by humiliating and punishing its pride. In verse fifteen, He addresses a third aspect of His judgment, which the next section will address.

In verse sixteen, God then addresses the consequences to Eve in two distinct ways. First, she will now suffer pain in childbirth. Anyone who has ever seen a birth knows the type of pain that comes with that action. Eve had yet to experience childbirth, so it is unknown what it would have looked like before the Fall, but now it will be a painful process. The word used for childbearing also focuses more on the entire process instead of just the birth; thus, for nine months, women will struggle with various pains, culminating in the birth of the child. Interestingly, the salvation promised in verse fifteen will come through the same childbirth process God cursed in verse sixteen.

Second, the text says two statements about Eve's relationship with Adam, "Your desire shall be for your husband, and he shall rule over you." Scholars disagree over what these statements mean. Some scholars see it as a physical desire for the husband that will overcome the challenges of the previous consequence. Even though it will hurt to go through childbearing, the woman will still desire to be with her husband. Others see it as more of a challenge, as she will be in constant strife with her husband and will challenge his authority. Either way, the consequences are that the path for deliverance, childbearing, will now be painful, and the relationship between husband and wife will be strained after the Fall.

Finally, verses 17-19 shift over to Adam as the final object of consequence. The first curse given to Adam is the curse of the ground. The Earth will no longer supply Adam with sustenance, probably as the garden had for his entire life. Instead, he would have to work hard to overcome the curse of sin. Thorns and thistles would come forth, and it would take immense labor to acquire the food needed for life. While man had tended the garden before the Fall, and thus labor was not entirely foreign for a perfect world, the curse of sin would make it much more challenging.

The consequence section ends with the promise of death for humanity. Just as God made Adam from the dust of the Earth, so too would he one day return to that dust. Hamilton argues that some commentators see this not as a consequence but as a relief from the tireless effort that Adam would have to make to survive, or even that death is not even in view in the passage.[15] While the idea that only death will stop the tireless nature of life, it is hard to ignore that God had already promised humanity back in 2:17 that sinful disobedience would lead to death. Whether Adam would have understood this as only physical death or if he understood the spiritual implications that Paul later described in Romans is unclear. Still, at the very least, Adam would have understood that physical death was now a consequence of the Fall.

God's Provisions (3:15, 21-24)

It seems as if humanity is doomed to wander the Earth, work tirelessly, and then die without any hope of reconciliation with God. However, in this dark time, God gave humanity three provisions after the Fall, two immediate and one long-term. He did not just come down to punish humankind but also to promise future redemption. The first immediate provision that God gives to Adam and Eve is a new wardrobe by giving them animal skins as clothes in verse twenty-one to replace the fig leaves that they had used to cover their shameful nakedness. Presumably, this is the first death in the text of Scripture.

Scholars disagree on whether this animal's death is the first sacrifice in the Bible. Walton writes, "It is a serious error to read sacrifice between the lines of verse twenty-one. The institution of sacrifice is far too significant an occurrence to leave it entirely to inference."[16] Hamilton writes, "It is probably reading too much into this verse to see in the coats of skin a hint of the use of animals in the sacrificial system of the OT cultus."[17] Walton argues that the clothes should be seen as God's provision since they are about to be driven out of the garden.[18]

Mathews argues in the other direction, arguing that the animal's death is the first sacrifice to cover sin. He writes, "Here God bestows "garments of skin" upon the guilty in the garden. Although the text does not specify that animals were slain to provide these coverings, it is a fair implication and one that likely would be made in the Mosaic community, where animal sacrifice was pervasive."[19] It does seem strange that if this is the first sacrifice, the text is not clearer. However, it does serve the purpose of covering humanity's sinful nakedness, just as the sacrificial system later would.

The provision continues uniquely in verses 22-24, as the passage introduces a new threat. There is a tree of life in the Garden of Eden that will allow humanity to live forever if eaten. God knows that if Adam and Eve eat from the Tree of Life, then they will live forever in their sinful condition. To protect them from an eternity of sin without hope of redemption, God must expel them from the garden and guard access to the Tree of Life with cherubim. Thus, while expulsion from the garden initially seems like a punishment for humanity, it is divine provision and blessing.

While the first two provisions immediately impact Adam and Eve, the final provision found in verse fifteen establishes a future provision. The verse, sometimes called the "Protoevangelium" or first gospel, has long been established in both Jewish and Christian thought as the first Messianic promise in the canon.[20] The passage begins with, "And I will put enmity between you and the woman, and between your seed and her Seed." The "you" refers to the serpent, as this verse's context is during the consequences for the serpent section. The passage continues, "He shall bruise your head, and you shall bruise His heel."

There is great debate within scholarship on the interpretation of this passage. Some scholars see it as a mythological story or reason humans fear snakes. Thus, the story has no supernatural elements but simply a myth created to explain a natural phenomenon. This view downplays the significance of the event. Within evangelicalism, two major interpretations have arisen: the humanity struggle view, which argues humanity will struggle against evil, and the Messianic view, which claims the Seed of the Woman represents the Messiah who will crush the power of Satan.

The first view is that this passage is not directly Messianic but instead argues that it is simply the idea that humanity will always struggle against the forces of evil. For example, John Walton writes,

> Throughout the church's history, this has been read as the first foreshadowing of Christ's defeat of Satan.... Given the repetition of the verb and the potentially mortal nature of both attacks, it becomes difficult to understand the verse as suggesting an eventual outcome to the struggle. Instead, both sides are exchanging potentially mortal blows of equal threat to the part of the body most vulnerable to their attack. The verse is depicting a continual, unresolved conflict between humans and the representatives of evil.[21]

This view has two principal arguments. First, as Walton noted, the verb used in the passage, usually translated as bruise or crush, is the same verb "יְשׁוּפְ" used in both instances. Therefore, the argument is that both the serpent's seed and the woman's seed are wounding each other with no clear winner. Some scholars have argued that the serpent is crushed on the head while the seed of the woman is wounded on the heel, but even a heel wound from a viper would kill the recipient. Second, holders of this position argue that the passage is never directly referenced in the rest of the Old Testament or the New Testament as a Messianic passage.

The second view holds that this passage refers to the future Messiah and establishes that He will one day have victory over the power of Satan. Four major arguments are used to defend this view. First, it is an ancient view within the church, dating back as far as Irenaeus. There is even some Jewish support for the view found in the Septuagint and the Targums.[22] Second, the passage and its context point to a Messianic interpretation. Sailhammer wrote, "Verse 15 thus contains a puzzling yet centrally important question: Who is the "seed" of the woman? The purpose of this verse is not to answer that question but to raise it. The remainder of the book of Genesis and the Pentateuch gives the author's answer."[23]

Hence, this verse sets the stage for the rest of the Messianic passages found throughout both the Pentateuch and the rest of the Old Testament. Seth Postel rightly asserts the connection as well between the seed in the passage and the continual use of seed throughout the rest of the book, writing, "It is little wonder, therefore, that "seed" becomes a keyword in the book of Genesis, and an ensuing conflict (at times mortal) between a chosen and rejected seed becomes its plot."[24]

Third, while the passage is never directly cited in the rest of the Old Testament or the New Testament as Messianic, it is alluded to in Romans 16:20, which states, "And the God of peace will crush Satan under your feet shortly." Pettus writes, "The apostle here apparently encourages the Roman church by reminding them that just as Christ, the seed of the woman, has 'crushed' Satan's head through his victory on the cross, he will also 'crush' the work of the enemy that is being directed against His 'seed' the church, presumably in the imminent eschaton."[25]

Fourth, the strongest argument for the Messianic interpretation is its necessity for humanity's hope. If the passage does not promise future judgment and victory, then it means that humanity would have been without hope for thousands of years until the time of Abraham. Would God have left humankind for centuries and generations without a possibility of hope? How would Adam, Enoch, or Noah have placed their hope and confidence in God and received salvation if God had not given them the possibility of a coming Savior? It seems much more probable, both textually and theologically, to view Genesis 3:15 as the first, albeit limited, promise of provision that God will fix the problem of evil and will one day defeat the power of sin and darkness. This promise is built on throughout the rest of the Old Testament and culminates in the coming of Jesus.

Theological Implications

No chapter in the Old Testament has the type of theological implications as Genesis chapter 3. The Fall of humanity into sin becomes the great challenge of the Bible, even more than the threat of Satan. Indeed, God does not destroy evil until the Great White Throne Judgment in Revelation 20.

Humanity has a sinful nature, and death is a reality in the universe. Work will be tough and tiresome. Childbearing will be a challenge and bring forth pain. It looked as if the world and humanity were doomed.

However, God provided. If there is a theme in the chapter, it is the provision of God. When humanity was naked, God clothed them. When humanity was in a precarious position with the possibility of extending a sinful condition, God provided. When humankind was dead in their sin and had no hope of redemption, God supplied them with a promise that one day, the Seed of the Woman would conquer the sinful world and defeat Satan. Jesus partially fulfilled this at His first coming. He died on the cross and rose again to beat the penalty of sin for humanity. Jesus will completely fulfill this promise at the Second Coming and defeat the forces of evil, as seen in Revelation 19-20. When humanity was at its lowest, lost, and needed a savior, God provided.

Application

Every believer needs God as a provider. We all need the salvation that God provided through Jesus' death and resurrection. However, we also need the provision of God in our lives every day. While we may not be naked and need clothes like Adam and Eve in the garden, we rely on God to provide for us daily. In Matthew 11:28-30, Jesus said, "Come to Me, all you who labor and are heavy laden, and I will give you rest. Take My yoke upon you and learn from Me, for I am gentle and lowly in heart, and you will find rest for your souls. For My yoke is easy and My burden is light." God wants us to ask for His provision, and He wants to help us in our lives. We must look to Him for provision and cast our cares to Him.

Conclusion

Let us return to our story from earlier about our magnificent desserts from our famous chef. We ended with us looking and smelling that delicious apple crumb streusel pie. Now, let's go further. Instead of just looking and smelling, we get a little friskier. When the chef turns his head, we sneak a bite of that delicious pie. We devour that piece of pie like it is the last on Earth. However, we quickly discover why the chef told us not to eat the pie. It is rotten on the inside. The apples were old, and the pit in our stomachs immediately started to feel the impact of eating the pie. A terrible bout of food poisoning is on its way, and there is nothing we can do to stop it.

Now, the chef turns around and sees what happened. He sees the missing piece of pie. He sees the remains of the crumbs and streusel on our hands and mouths. What would be his response? He could and should say, "What have you done? I told you not to eat that! You will be sick now." He could be disgusted and leave us to suffer the consequences of our actions. But what if he did not? What if he said, "Look, I told you not to eat that pie. I told you that because I was trying to protect you from the consequences of eating the pie. However, now that you have eaten the pie, I cannot completely remove those consequences. But I will take you to the doctor. I will get you medicine that will help your food-poisoned stomach. I will take you home and get you into bed. I will stay and make sure that you are okay. I will make you crackers and ensure you fully recover from this sickness." We would be lucky to have a chef who would be that generous to us when we completely ignored his warnings. In the same way, we are fortunate to have a God who provided for us in our darkest times instead of leaving us in our sinful, rotten condition. God came down to provide for us when we were at our lowest. We did not earn it. We did not deserve it. But God loves us, and God provides for us.

Chapter Two

Tower of Babel: Judgment

But the LORD came down to see the city   Genesis 11:5

I have had the privilege of being a professor at a university for several years. One of the significant challenges of being a professor, at least for me, is getting students to complete their work. Growing up and going to school and then college, I was a tenacious student. I finished my work on time and usually completed it several days early, especially if it was a significant project/assignment. Therefore, when I started teaching, I assumed most students would be like me. I was wrong. Unbelievably, most college students like to procrastinate. Some students are good at procrastination. They can wait until the last minute and still complete the assignment well. Others, not so much. They either submit an unfinished project or wait to turn it in late. While I want to see the students succeed, it is at this point that judgment must fall.

Genesis 11:1-9 tells the story of the Tower of Babel, one of the most famous stories in the Bible. It is also a story that many readers often misunderstand. It is not simply a story about people who did not want to get lost, so they built a large tower. Instead, it is a story about a people who refuse to listen to the plans of God and try to reject and manipulate God. Through these events, God comes down and judges the people for rejecting His ways.

Immediate Context

Scholars traditionally divide the Book of Genesis into chapters 1-11 and 12-50. Thus, chapter eleven serves as both the culmination of the events of chapters 1-11 and the connection bridge between the book's two sections. 11:1-9 is found right in the middle of this divide. Before the passage, in chapter ten, God divided the nations after the impact of the great flood. After this section, the book starts to zoom in on the family line of Abram, connecting this chapter not only with chapter twelve but with the story of the patriarchs that make up the rest of Genesis.

The key interpretive issue in the structure of this section is whether the events of Genesis 11:1-9 occurred before, during, or after the events established in chapter 10. Why is the chronology significant? In chapter ten, God divided the nations, and various people groups seem to have their unique languages. However, the events in chapter eleven have only one language available until after the Tower of Babel event. The two stories contradict. Therefore, many scholars have argued that the events of chapter eleven occur out of chronological order and instead explain how the events of chapter ten ultimately occurred. For example, Mathews writes, "After portraying the postdiluvian world as made up of related but "scattered" nations (10:5, 18b,

32), the Babel story explains the reason for the dispersed setting (11:4, 8–9). The initial breakup of the postdiluvian people was achieved by the muddling of their language, which foiled the ambitions of the human family."[26] Hence, one should not be confused when moving from chapter ten to chapter eleven and wondering what happened in the world; instead, one should view it as an explanation for why the events happened.

The Setup (11:1-2)

Chapter eleven opens with a setup for the story of Babel in two ways. First, it established that there was only one language. This unique period in history is almost incomprehensible for a modern reader who lives in a world with over 7,000 languages. Indeed, when one travels to a different country or even a distinct region in many countries, there is a different language. Scholars differ on what it means when the text makes this statement, especially given that chapter ten had already established that various people groups had different languages (10:5, 20, 31). Some scholars argue that the final events of chapter ten occurred after the Tower of Babel incident. Thus, the world at this time only had one language.[27] Other scholars, such as Victor Hamilton, argue that different cultures had different languages but that there was a lingua franca, a common language everyone shared alongside their languages.[28] While both options are possible, the first option is the more likely option based on the events of Chapter 11, as will be addressed later in the chapter.

Second, the text states that a group of people moved to the east and ended up in a plain on the land of Shinar. The question that arises is, who is this group of people? Is it the world's entire population then, or is it simply a smaller subset of the population? Some of this depends on where one places the events of chapter eleven chronologically, either before, during, or after chapter ten. Also, the idea of the whole earth is vague. Mathews writes,

> Commentators are divided on the geographical extent meant by "whole world." If it is taken at face value, our passage speaks comprehensively of the world's populations. Others view it as a figure of speech (hyperbole) or better translated "all the land," limiting it to the Mesopotamian region. The Hebrew phrase may be used in Genesis and the Old Testament both to designate a limited region and also the whole earth. Since the author has tied the Babel event to the Table of Nations, which exceeds the boundaries of a given region, it would be best to understand the expression in its broader application—at least in the sense of the world known to the author.[29]

The best conclusion would be that this group is either the entire population of the earth at this time or, at the very least, a substantial portion of the population large enough to impact the whole region of the Ancient Near East.

The fact that the group ended up in the land of Shinar is not a coincidence. Shinar was the ancient name for Mesopotamia, specifically Babylon (Daniel 1:2). The author of Genesis already listed this region in 10:8-10 as the region where Nimrod established his kingdom. Babylon went on to be one of the major players throughout history, culminating in the Neo-Babylonian Empire that would conquer Jerusalem, destroy the first temple, and lead the Jews into exile. John uses the name again in the Book of Revelation to signify the power and religious perversion of the Antichrist.

The Problem of the Tower (3:3-4)

Verse three builds on the setup from verses 1-2, stating, "Then they said to one another, "Come, let us make bricks and bake them thoroughly." They had brick for stone, and they had asphalt for mortar." The idea of building bricks makes sense, given the location of Shinar or future Babylon. The region of Babylon was void of natural resources, especially lumber or stone. Therefore, they had to use other types of resources in construction, such as fired brick. Walton describes this process in detail,

> The alluvial plains of southern Mesopotamia had no stone available. Anyone using stones had to transport them many miles, an expensive proposition. As a result, as early as the Late Uruk Period at the end of the fourth millennium B.C., we see the development of kiln-fired brick. Furthermore, as the text indicates, the usual mortar used with kiln-fired brick was a bitumen-based mastic. This combination of baked brick and bitumen mastic made for waterproof buildings as sturdy as stone. The time required to fire the bricks and to procure the bitumen made this an expensive procedure. As a result, only the most important buildings were constructed with these materials.[30]

This technology was standard throughout Babylonian history. Indeed, the brick kiln or something similar was probably the furnace used in Daniel 3 with Shadrack, Meshack, and Abednego thousands of years later.

The idea of making bricks also has a strong connection with the Book of Exodus. Pharaoh commanded the Israelites to make bricks for his empire in Exodus 5:7-8.[31] Brickmaking was a common practice throughout the ancient Near East. As seen in the text of Exodus, enslaved people or members of the lowest social classes were usually the ones who practiced this profession. Could this be the first hint of slavery or oppression in the text? It certainly is a strong possibility.

In Verse Four, the author notes that the people would build a city and a tower with these bricks. What exactly does the text mean when it describes a tower? It is unlikely that the tower was a type of skyscraper as sometimes portrayed in children's books. It was likely a type of early ziggurat. Ziggurat's were

> A structure that was built to support a stairway. This stairway was a visual representation of that which was believed to be used by the gods to travel from one realm to another. It was solely for the convenience of the gods and was maintained in order to provide the deity with the amenities that would refresh him along the way. At the top of the ziggurat was the gate of the gods, the entrance into their heavenly abode. At the bottom was the temple, where hopefully the God would descend to receive the gifts and worship of his people.[32]

Thus, they were building a city and a religious structure that would allow them to access their gods in some capacity.

The reasons given in the text for the creation of this town and tower were, "Let us make a name for ourselves, lest we be scattered abroad over the face of the whole earth" (11:3). As will be seen later in the chapter, God views this negatively. However, there is much scholarly debate on why God was upset with the creation of the city/tower and the reasons for the creation, culminating in three different views. The first view is simply that the people rejected the mandate given to them in 9:1 about multiplying over the earth, either from fear or pride. For example, Ross writes, "Here the people came together to strengthen themselves and in pride to make a reputation for themselves lest they be scattered over the face of the whole earth. This rebellion opposes God's command to spread and fill the entire world."[33] Thus, God was angry because the people had rejected His commands to cover the earth and had instead gathered in one location.

A second view is that there was more religious motivation for the tower's construction. Walton writes,

> Ziggurat function assumes a particular concept of God—a function that is at the root of the Babylonian religious system. In fact, it is fair to say that the ziggurat was the most powerful representation of the Babylonian religious system, a system in which the gods were recast with human natures… In other words, with the development of urbanization people began to envision their gods in human terms. People were no longer trying to be like God, but more insidiously, were trying to bring God down to the level of fallen humanity.[34]

Thus, in Walton's view, "The offense in this passage, then, is to be found in the beliefs that resulted in the project and what it stood for in the minds of the builders. It went beyond mere idolatry; it degraded the nature of God by portraying him as having needs."[35]

A third view is that what is happening in the text is the creation of the foundations of an empire. The people were not just creating a city to live in but a fortress to establish themselves as the dominant people in the ancient world. The idea of making a name for themselves was not simply about building the city itself but the empire that would come about because of the city. Hamilton writes, "the builders also thought that the existence of a fortified city would be the guarantee of their security."[36] Indeed, when the text describes the tower as having "whose top is in the heavens," it does not necessarily mean that they were thinking about the realm of the gods.

Deuteronomy 1:28 used similar language, "the cities *are* great and fortified up to heaven," to describe the walled cities of Canaan when the twelve spies entered the land. It is evident in that passage that the spies were not describing the towns in any religious sense but in the idea that they were mighty fortresses that would be difficult to overcome militarily. In Jeremiah 51:53, Jeremiah used similar language to describe the invulnerability of Babylon. Creating a city that would lead to an empire like this would have made a name or a reputation for its builders.

All three views have their strengths and weaknesses. However, option three has some strong arguments in its favor, especially if the idea of making bricks brings the concept of slavery or oppression, something that empires were well known for throughout the Ancient Near East. However, regardless of which view one takes, the primary issue that all three have in common is the issue of pride. The people wanted to make a name for themselves, and therefore, they did what they did because of the pride of humanity. The sin of pride that we see in Genesis 3 with the fall of man continues with the construction of the Tower of Babel.

God's Observation (11:5-6)

Verse five begins God's response to the creation of the Tower of Babel. The text states, "But the LORD came down to see the city and the tower which the sons of men had built." God did not have to physically come down from heaven to know what the people were doing. God is omniscient and knows everything. The point of the verse was that God was once again intervening in human history. While God can intervene from His heavenly throne, He has taken a more direct role at various times in history. He was "coming down" from His heavenly abode to see what humanity once again was up to, very similar to when He came down in the garden after the initial fall of man in chapter three.

Verse six then establishes the why behind God's response. He states, "Indeed the people are one, and they all have one language, and this is what they begin to do; now nothing they propose to do will be withheld from them." Regarding the three views mentioned earlier, they all vary slightly in terms of what exactly God views as the problem. In view one, the problem was simply pride and disobedience. Thus, when God came down to see what was happening, He saw people ignoring His commands to fill the earth.

The second view would see the issue in a much more religious/idolatrous manner. The people tried to make the gods into their images through need and necessity. Indeed, both the Bible and History are filled with examples of idolatry. People were constantly trying to feed the gods through their idols, build homes for the gods with their temples, and make sacrifices to the gods to please them. If this was a move to idolatry through the ziggurat system, then God knew that this was just the start and that the people would never stop trying to humanize the gods, leading to the types of idolatrous systems built throughout history.

In view three, God would see the issue with the imperial state's creation and the oppression it brings. God was certainly not against nations, as He was the one to establish nations and various people groups throughout history. Indeed, He even created a specific nation, Israel, to accomplish His purposes. However, the Bible makes it clear that God was not in favor of the types of empires established throughout history because they tended to oppress their neighbors and do terrible things to those that they conquered. Egypt would become the first example of God's judgment on empires through the story of the Exodus. The prophets make this clear later in history. God would judge Assyria for their wickedness, then Babylon. Daniel even describes the judgments of Greece and probably Rome. Consequently, while God established the nations, He would not allow a nation to become a tyrant, overpowering other nations with sinful actions without suffering divine judgment. If God had allowed the people to build this city and fortress and allowed the people to become an oppressive empire, especially this early in history when they would have no legitimate rival, then they could have conquered and subjugated the known world.

God's Judgment on Babel (11:7-9)

Verse seven outlined God's plan to eliminate this problem. The "let us" statement, like Genesis 1:26, has divided scholars for centuries. Is this passage a hidden reference to the Trinity? Is it a passage about God and His angels or a divine council? It is beyond the scope of this book to deal with that issue in detail, but regardless, God Himself will intervene with judgment on humanity for their actions and to limit the damage done by the construction project.

God's judgment was not destroying the town and the tower but instead confusing the people's languages. If God had destroyed the city, then they could have tried to rebuild. Instead, God made it impossible to continue with the project. Presumably, because the text was extremely limited on how this occurred, the people building could no longer effectively communicate with each other. In a way, it serves as a counter to the Day of Pentecost, when the disciples were able to communicate effectively to people of all types of languages (Acts 2). God must have created new languages at this point so that the confusion would have an impact. They could quickly translate the languages to continue communication if they had already established languages. However, if God had given them new languages, then it would have taken years for anyone to be able to communicate with each other effectively.

Verse eight then establishes the ultimate consequence of the judgment. The people were scattered all over the face of the earth. Whether or not this was the scattering described in chapter ten is not definitive. Still, it does seem to be related to that scattering, especially in 10:25 and 10:32. The other significant consequence occurs at the end of verse eight, "and they ceased building the city." God's judgment had been practical. They could no longer finish their project, and God's judgment halted the construction. Regardless of which position was taken earlier, the judgment had limited the scope of damage that could have come from the completion of the town. Verse nine ends the story with the connection of the place called Babel, translated "as confusion." The people thought that they would make a name for themselves with their construction, and instead, all that they ended up with was divine confusion.

Theological Implications

There are three significant theological implications in this passage. The first is that pride leads to man's downfall. Pride was involved regardless of which position one takes of why the people built the town and the tower. The people wanted to make a name for themselves. They thought they could do something incredible that would make them a name throughout the land and history. However, the Bible is clear that selfish pride is in direct contrast to the ways of God. Proverbs 8:13 states that God hates pride. Throughout the Bible, God constantly humbles the proud: the building of Babel, the Pharoah of the Exodus, Sennacherib, Nebuchadnezzar, Herod, and even Satan himself. The building of Babel continues a protracted line of prideful falls that began in the Garden of Eden and continued throughout the rest of Scripture.

A second theological emphasis is that humanity's kings, kingdoms, and empires are ultimately doomed to fail, especially when they are established in the ways of the fallen world instead of the ways of God. The people established the kingdom of Babel on pride and a desire to make itself great. Many empires have continued this same trajectory, and like Babel, all have fallen. Humanity should never put its faith or trust in a kingdom to deliver them instead of God. Indeed, only one kingdom in the Bible is described as having no end. In Daniel 2:44, after Daniel described the fall of the major kingdoms of Ancient Near Eastern history (Babylon, Persia, Greece, and Rome), he described a final kingdom. He told Nebuchadnezzar "And in the days of these kings the God of heaven will set up a kingdom which shall never be destroyed; and the kingdom shall not be left to other people; it shall break in pieces and consume all these kingdoms, and it shall stand forever." God's kingdom alone, with the Messiah

Jesus at the helm, will be the only kingdom in history never to be defeated and to guarantee victory and salvation for its members.

A final theological implication in this chapter is God's patience in judgment. At any point in the story of the construction of Babel, God could have wiped out the builders with divine judgment. However, He showed patience and grace in the event, instead enacting confusion on the people to stop the construction rather than outright destruction. While there are times in the Bible where God does send direct judgment that kills and destroys, such as at Sodom and Gomorrah, in most cases, God is patient and gives multiple opportunities for humanity to change, such as Jonah's sermon to Nineveh or His patience with the people of Israel throughout their history. Many times, readers of the Old Testament will talk about the judgment of God and try to frame it as if He is a terrible, vengeful deity. However, much of the Old Testament shows the exact opposite; He is a patient and loving God who gives second chances, many times significantly more than the average person would in the same situation.

Application

Proverbs 18:16 states, "Pride goes before destruction, and a haughty spirit before a fall." As seen earlier in the theological implications section, pride served as one of the significant downfalls in the story of Babel and the downfall of many throughout both the Old and New Testaments. Similarly, pride is still a considerable sin issue today. If we are not careful, we can let pride lead us to envy and jealousy. How often do we sin and wonder how we got here? The answer is that pride, envy, and jealousy frequently open the door to other sins.

These sins can even happen in the ministry. Many pastors have become too prideful of the size and power of their churches, only to see that pride lead to their downfall. Others have been envious of more prominent churches with more notable buildings and budgets and do not accept the place God has put them in, leading to frustration in ministry. Pride can tear even the most faithful Christian down if left unchecked and is something we all need to be on guard against in our daily walks with Christ.

A second area of application that we can see in this chapter is "making a name for ourselves." We often hear the concept of "legacy," which is biblical. Even the idea of having a "name be great" is not necessarily a negative idea, as in the next chapter of Genesis in chapter twelve, God promised that very thing for Abram. Thus, creating a Godly legacy is something that we should strive for in our lives.

The problem of making a name for us is when we try to do this outside God's will and mission. In this passage, the builders of Babel were not creating a tower and city to glorify God but to glorify themselves. When we go outside God's plan and will and decide to make things about ourselves, we will fail.

However, when we build a legacy for God, He will often bless us and give us a legacy in the world that will also last beyond us, just as He did with people like Abraham, Moses, David, or Paul.

Conclusion

Let us return to our procrastinating students. Sometimes, I get emails from students asking for extensions for their assignments the night before something is due. If there is a legitimate need for an extension, say a sickness or emergency, etc. I will, at times, give out that extension. However, when it comes to procrastination and students saying that they need more time on the assignment because they were too busy or they just waited too long to start on it, I usually do not grant the extension but instead, enforce the late penalty on the assignment, the judgment so to speak. Some might ask, "Dr. Sloan, why are you so strict about enforcing these rules and deadlines? Shouldn't you show a little grace to your students?"

However, my thought process is that I am helping to prepare these students for the working world. I even tell my students going into the ministry that their congregations will not attend on Tuesday to hear their sermons. Sure, I could give the students extensions, and I hope that one day, they will learn to correct their mistakes in planning and preparation. But I am not doing my job to prepare them if I condone their actions. Sometimes, when mistakes or errors happen, judgment must occur as well.

Just as I love my students and want them to succeed, God loves humanity and wants us to grow. Nevertheless, when humanity makes mistakes and rebels against the plans and commands of God, there are times when God must come down and bring judgment to humankind. It does not mean that God does not love us. It does not mean that God is a mean and vengeful God. Instead, God is a loving God who does not want humanity to continue in its sinful condition and, therefore, judges humankind in a manner that will hopefully lead it back to repentance and obedience.

Chapter Three

The Exodus: Deliverance

I am come down to deliver them Exodus 3:7-8

As a kid, you can sometimes get into challenging situations that are impossible to escape. When I was a kid, my older brother and I went to the store to buy a new video game. When we got home, the video game did not work. This event was when you could not buy a digital download and still had to buy the disk. We immediately put the disk back into the case and returned to the store to exchange the game for a new disk since it was not working. However, when we got to the store, the clerk said that because we had opened the game, he would not accept it back for a refund or exchange. My brother and I did not know what to do in this situation; we were just kids. What should we do when an adult tells us he would not exchange the game? We needed a deliverer to come in and save us in this situation.

The story of the Exodus is one of the most well-known stories in the world's history. Even Hollywood has made several movies about it. It is the ultimate story of God's deliverance in the Old Testament. The people of Israel were in dire straits, and it took God coming down to deliver them.

Immediate Context

The story of the Exodus began not in the Book of Exodus but in Genesis 15. In this chapter, God told Abram that his descendants would number as the stars of the heavens and that these descendants would one day inherit the Promised Land (15:4-8). However, verses 13-14 in this chapter also describe that Abram's descendants would "be strangers in a land that is not theirs, and will serve them, and they will afflict them four hundred years" but that eventually "the nation whom they serve I will judge; afterward they shall come out with great possessions." While chapter fifteen did not identify which nation would enslave Abram's descendants, the end of the Book of Genesis leads the story into Egypt through the story of Joseph.

The Book of Exodus then picked up the story after the death of Joseph. A new king who did not know Joseph arose over Egypt and enslaved Abraham's descendants (1:8-14). This enslavement occurred for hundreds of years, just as God had predicted to Abram. Chapter two of Exodus then introduces the character of Moses. This child, saved miraculously from death as a baby and put into the house of the Pharaoh, would become a prince of Egypt, even as a native Israelite. However, Moses went out to see his people in slavery and intervened when he saw an Egyptian beating a Hebrew slave, killing the Egyptian in the process. Once Pharaoh learned about the killing, he sought to kill Moses, who fled to Midian. At Midian, Moses met Zipporah, married her, and had a child named Gershom.

Chapter two ended with a break in the story of Moses and went back to the events in Egypt. Verse 23 described that the king of Egypt, the Pharaoh who tried to kill Moses and forced him to flee, had passed away. The verse continued by describing the situation of the Israelites, that they were groaning in their bondage and were crying out to God for deliverance. The chapter concluded with God hearing the cries of His people, remembering the covenant He had made with Abram and his descendants, and acknowledging them and their situation.[37] Thus, the stage was set for God to intervene and deliver the Israelites from their bondage, just as He had promised Abram hundreds of years prior. However, the question that arises in the text is, how? Chapter three will answer that question through Moses's call.

Encountering a Burning Bush in the Desert (3:1-6)

Chapter three of Exodus begins in verse one. It sets the stage for the chapter, stating, "Now Moses was tending the flock of Jethro his father-in-law, the priest of Midian. And he led the flock to the back of the desert, and came to Horeb, the mountain of God" (3:1). Inherent in the "now" of the text was a roughly forty-year time gap between the events of chapter two and the beginning of chapter three, as seen in Acts 7:23 and 7:30. Moses had been living in Midian for about half of his life, a fugitive on the run from Pharaoh for his actions in Egypt. He was most likely unaware that the Pharaoh had died, as established at the end of chapter two.

Moses was also a shepherd, tending the flock of his father-in-law, Jethro. Stuart points out that this occupation shows that Moses is now identifying himself with his Jewish heritage over his Egyptian upbringing. Genesis had identified that Egyptians loathed shepherds, which is why Joseph had told his brothers to tell the Egyptians that they were shepherds since the Egyptians viewed shepherds as an "abomination" (Genesis 46:33). Stuart writes, "Moses' identification with his ethnic people was now so strong that he was willing to serve in the occupation of a shepherd, an assignment that no one who still thought of himself as an Egyptian would ever have taken on."[38] Moses also shepherded Jethro's flocks, which may show that he was working with or even for his father-in-law. Thus, the mighty prince of Egypt was now a simple shepherd who did not even have a herd for himself. Hence, Durham sums it up well when he writes, "At the beginning of the account of the most momentous experience of his life, Moses is presented not only as not seeking such an experience but as totally oblivious to the possibility of the confrontation that is to follow."[39]

Moses was driving toward Horeb through this shepherding moment, identified in the text as the "mountain of God." It is unlikely that Horeb was known as the mountain of God at this point.⁴⁰ Indeed, Kaiser argues, "He goes so far that he comes to "Horeb, the mountain of God." This designation does not mean that the mountain is a well-known cultic spot; rather, the term is used proleptically of that spot that will become well known to both Moses and his listeners (readers) by the time the narrative is written."⁴¹ Indeed, nothing in the text would hint that Moses was actually moving to this mountain to encounter God, but that God chose this location to meet Moses instead. This location will become known as the "mountain of God" after Moses' interaction and the Israelites' interaction later in the book when they arrive at this location to receive the laws of God.

The story then shifts in verses two and three, "And the Angel of the LORD appeared to him in a flame of fire from the midst of a bush. So he looked, and behold, the bush was burning with fire, but the bush was not consumed. Then Moses said, "I will now turn aside and see this great sight, why the bush does not burn." Moses, doing something he had probably done almost every day for forty years, suddenly saw something that caught his attention: a bush was on fire but not burning. Stuart asserts that this would have stood out to Moses because, as a shepherd, he would have known how to keep warm on cold nights in the wilderness and would have been aware of how quickly bushes would have burned in these conditions.⁴²

Moses did not realize that the "Angel of the Lord" was in the fire in the middle of the bush. Therefore, the fire was not natural but divine, a fire made to get his attention and draw him to the presence of God. The presence of God seen in fire is a theme consistent throughout the Bible. The pillar of fire of the Exodus, the fire in the Tabernacle and the Temple, and even the tongues of fire with the coming of the Holy Spirit are just a few examples of God's presence being associated with fire.

The identity of the Angel of the Lord is a hotly debated issue within scholarship. Some view the being as simply an angel that God sends out. Others view the being as God Himself, either as God the Father or a pre-incarnate Jesus. Stuart argues that the being must be associated with God in some manner as the being is identified as both Lord (vv. 2, 4, 7, 15, 16, 18) and God (vv. 4–6, 11–16, 18).⁴³ Given the nature of the Old Testament text, it is difficult to know whether the being can definitively be associated with a pre-incarnate Jesus. Still, it does seem that the being is associated with God and God's presence.

Verse four then establishes the beginning of their communication. God, upon seeing He had Moses' attention, called out to him twice. Stuart argues, "In ancient Semitic culture, addressing someone by saying his or her name twice was a way of expressing endearment, affection and friendship. Thus, Moses would have understood immediately that he was being addressed by someone who loved him and was concerned about him".⁴⁴ Moses answers God with the simple Hebrew word *"Hineni,"* translated as "here I am." This answer is used throughout the Old Testament to respond to the call of God. Abraham used it in Genesis 22:1 to answer to God in the story of the sacrifice of Isaac. Jacob answered God with the word in Genesis 46:2. Samuel answered God with this word in 1 Samuel 3:4 when God called out to him about the future of Eli and his sons. Isaiah answered the call of God in Isaiah 6:8 with this word. Indeed, *"Hineni"* is used throughout the Old Testament as the answer to God's call.

In verse five, God gives Moses two commands. First, he was not to get any closer to the burning bush. Kaiser argues, "This is to prevent him from rashly intruding into God's presence and to teach him that God is separate and distinct from mortal human beings " (cf. 19: 10– 13; 2Pe 1: 18)."[45] Second, he tells Abraham to take off his sandals because he is standing on holy ground. The ground itself, Horeb, was not holy ground by itself. It was only considered holy ground because of God's presence through the burning bush. God's presence creates holy ground, be it the Tabernacle, the temple, or the burning bush.

The section of the chapter ends with God connecting Himself with the God of Moses' ancestors. He begins with, "I am the God of your father." Moses' father is first mentioned in chapter two, although he is unnamed in that passage. Later passages identify his name as Amram. God continued by stating He was the "God of Abraham, the God of Isaac, and the God of Jacob". Thus, as Wright argues, the point is clearly to establish the single continuous identity of this living God across the generations.[46] The God before Moses is the same God who interacted with his ancestors hundreds of years ago. Indeed, the mention of Abraham, Isaac, and Jacob may contain an allusion to the covenant promises given to the nation, promises that Moses and the Israelites had probably assumed would never happen based on their current circumstances.[47] Once Moses realized who he was interacting with, he hid his face in fear, a standard action in the presence of the Lord throughout the Bible. It is easy to think that Moses' mind was racing with two questions: why was the God of his ancestors here, and what did He want with a fugitive shepherd?

I Have Come Down (3:7-10)

Verse seven serves for Moses as a recap of 2:24-25. The reader has already seen God's acknowledgment of His people, but now Moses would understand as well that God had seen and was about to respond to the sufferings of His people. Garrett argues that what God was doing was "drawing Moses into the heavenly perspective on Israel's enslavement, allowing Moses to, as it were, sit beside God as he sees the suffering of his people."[48] Moses was already familiar with this suffering. Indeed, he had even tried to stop the suffering forty years ago, which had made him a fugitive. However, by hearing what God Himself had seen, heard, and knew their sorrows, Moses now understood that he wasn't the only being who understood the predicament of the Israelites.

However, just understanding that God knew of the predicament of His people did not automatically mean that God would intervene. After all, for all that Moses knew, God had seen His people suffering for hundreds of years in bondage and yet had not intervened on their behalf. It is unknown how much Moses knew about Israel's history at this time. Did he know the promise that God had made to Abraham centuries ago? The text is not clear. However, verse eight goes one step further; God had "come down to deliver them out of the hand of the Egyptians" (3:8). How exactly God will do this was not addressed in this verse but will be addressed later in the passage.

The second half of verse eight expanded upon God's message of deliverance. It would be one thing to get the nation out of slavery in Egypt. However, the nation would still be homeless without the land promised to them hundreds of years ago through the Abrahamic Covenant. God said, "And to bring them up from that land to a good and large land, to a land flowing with milk and honey, to the place of the Canaanites and the Hittites and the Amorites and the Perizzites and the Hivites and the Jebusites" (3:8).

Wright identifies a U-shaped pattern to the narrative. God comes down into Egypt so that He can bring the people up into the land He had promised them.[49] God was not simply promising them deliverance but also the completion of a promise of a homeland. While Moses, at this point, may not have understood the implications of these words, that conquest would be necessary and much work would still need to be done, ultimately, what mattered was that God would be with the nation and was guaranteeing that they would experience the blessing of the Promised Land. Alexander notes the personality in the passage, stating, "The repeated use of "I" underscores God's personal commitment to this project, and twice he refers to the Israelites as "my people."[50]

Verse nine replicates the message of verse seven. Then, the section ends with verse ten, which states, "Come now, therefore, and I will send you to Pharaoh that you may bring My people, the children of Israel, out of Egypt" (3:10). This was probably not the message that Moses had expected. When God said He would come down, Moses probably assumed he was off the hook. God would intervene on behalf of the Israelites, and Moses could stay in Midian and pretend that the burning bush incident had never happened.

Instead, God was telling Moses that not only would Moses be involved in the deliverance of his people but would also be the one to confront Pharaoh and lead his people out of slavery. He would have to go face to face with one of the most powerful men in the world, the Pharaoh of Egypt himself.[51] Indeed, this verse commissions Moses as the human agent who will serve as God's representative.[52] God was commissioning Moses to complete the mission

Moses thought he could undertake so many years before his exile. The question in the text is whether Moses is still willing to answer the call.

Answering the Call or Excusing the Call (3:11-17)

If God was expecting Moses to answer the call with an affirmative immediately, He certainly did not get that response. Instead of saying yes, he attempts to get more information. He sought answers from God with two questions: "Who am I that I should go to Pharaoh, and that I should bring the children of Israel out of Egypt?" (3:11). Scholars disagree on whether this initial response from Moses was one of mild rejection of God's call, believing that he was the wrong man for the job, or if it was simply a cultural response to God.

Stuart takes the second approach, arguing that Moses was not denying God in any way but simply using a cultural custom. He writes,

> Moses' "Who am I?" is a *pro forma* question, not an expression of lack of self-confidence. At this point, at least, he was not trying to get out of the job Yahweh was calling him to perform but was being mannerly according to the dictates of his culture. The exact expression, "Who am I" occurs two other times in the Old Testament, in each instance as part of expressing polite acceptance of an honor rather than as an attempt to decline it.[53]

Stuart also argues that what Moses was doing in this case was expressing his humility in this manner.[54] Thus, he wasn't denying God's power or ability to use him as much as showing humility before an all-powerful God.

Others take an approach that allows for more rejection/questioning of God's selection. Garrett argues that Moses was asserting that he was inadequate for the task.[55] Kaiser also argues that Moses was too timid and not the same man he was as a younger man. He writes, "He was only too eager to offer himself as a self-styled deliverer prior to this extended training in Midian, but at this point Moses presents a different problem to the Lord. He is now timid, unsure of himself, and shrinks back from any self-assertiveness that his divine commission demands of him."[56] While Moses clearly showed humility to God, it does seem that he was, at the very least, hesitant to answer this call, much more hesitant than he would have been forty years prior.

If Moses was hesitant or mildly rejecting God's call, he certainly had a couple of good reasons to do this, which he put forth. Initially, he brought up the idea of going to see Pharaoh. Moses could have been thinking of this for two primary reasons. First, he was a fugitive on the run from the Egyptians. Indeed, Moses had left Egypt forty years before as a wanted man. He had no real way of knowing at this point that he would not immediately be arrested and possibly killed for his previous crimes.[57] Second, Moses probably thought he had no authority in the eyes of Pharaoh. He was not a prince of Egypt anymore. Moses was not a king of another rival empire. He was a simple shepherd from Midian.

Moses then brought up his second reason: that the Israelites would not listen to him. Alexander says, "Since his childhood Moses had lived apart from his own people, initially in the Egyptian court and more recently in the land of Midian."[58] Outside of possibly his immediate family, with whom he had some type of relationship since they had raised him initially (2:9), Moses would have been viewed as an Egyptian by most of his brethren. Even if they accepted him as one of their own, they probably still would have had no reason to think that God had somehow empowered him to get them out of slavery. He was a fugitive shepherd from a distant land, not a leader within the nation.

At this point, Kaiser brings up an interesting observation about Moses' responses. He writes, "It is strange that Moses does not raise another, larger issue— the feasibility of organizing, equipping, and sustaining such a massive escape."[59] Indeed, he did not seem to question whether or not God could allow for this Exodus, but that he was the wrong choice to be able to lead the event. Perhaps the miracle of the burning bush or even the stories of God that he had heard as a small child had impacted him to the point that he believed God could bring forth this Exodus. His only objection was that God had picked the wrong man for the job.

In verse twelve, God began to answer Moses' objections. He could have told Moses that He had been preparing Moses to be this chosen deliverer since birth. Instead, God said, "I will certainly be with you." Stuart sees this simple phrase as an answer to both objections. He writes, "For God to 'be with' someone means that he provides that person direct, special help and guidance that, in turn, can cause people to recognize that person's worth and/or authority in given situations."[60] Thus, God's presence with Moses would not only empower Moses to deliver his people but also empower him to know that God had selected Moses to accomplish this task, both in the presence of Pharaoh and the people of Israel. Truly, when Moses entered Pharaoh's presence in chapter five, Pharaoh did not question who Moses was or why he was there but instead only questioned who God was.

God then gave Moses a sign to seal His promise that He would be with Moses. He told Moses, "And this shall be a sign to you that I have sent you: When you have brought the people out of Egypt, you shall serve God on this mountain." This sign was very different than a traditional sign given upon the call of a prophet/deliverer. Usually, the sign was given to them that could be fulfilled before their calling so they could have confidence that God would be with them. Moses received some of these signs later in chapter four.

Instead, this sign was what Alexander calls a fulfillment sign; Moses must trust and obey God first to see it fulfilled.[61] It is almost as if the sign itself is a bit of an afterthought because if the Israelites were free and able to worship God on Mount Sinai, God had intervened and delivered them. Kaiser also argues that the sign shows a deeper spiritual meaning. He writes, "There is also more than a hint in this sign that the mission of Moses goes beyond a mere deliverance of a nation from bondage; Israel is to be set free to "worship" God."[62] Stuart similarly writes, "They would get to Sinai, but more importantly, they would get to saving belief in the only true and living God."[63] Hence, Moses' task was not simply to free the Israelites from their enslavement but also to bring them back to the God who had been with their forefathers, the same God who had promised them deliverance back in Genesis 15. The Exodus event then became not just a physical deliverance for the nation but also a spiritual deliverance.

In verse thirteen, Moses asked God a very pointed question. If he was going to do this mission that God had called him to do when the Israelites asked him who sent him or gave him this authority and he said God did, he assumed they would ask, "What is His name?' what shall I say to them?" Garret views this as a pagan idea. He writes, "The question, "What is his name?" suggests a pagan outlook. In Egypt, every god had a name that identified the deity by gender, cult location, powers, specialized tasks, and rank within the hierarchy of deities.[64] While this is not definitive in the text, there is clearly a sense of either pagan pluralism or at least a bit of vagueness in that Moses wonders if the people will automatically assume that the God who sent him was the same God of their ancestors.

Verse fourteen famously gives God's answer to Moses: "And God said to Moses, "I AM WHO I AM." And He said, "Thus you shall say to the children of Israel, 'I AM has sent me to you.'" The Hebrew translation of this statement is notoriously complicated. For example, Kaiser writes, "On the etymology and meaning of the name Yahweh, there is almost no agreement. The bibliography in the last century alone would fill a whole book, and there seems to be no end in sight."[65] Ross sums up the translation well when she states,

> The idea that the "I AM" in Exod. 3 reveals God as the Being who is absolutely self-existent, and who, in Himself, possesses essential life and permanent existence. To the Hebrew, to be does not just mean to exist, but to be active, to express oneself in active being. God is the One who acts. The "I AM" or "I will be" is God's promise that He will redeem the children of Israel."[66]

Therefore, the name given to Moses was not simply God's name, usually translated YHWH or Yahweh, but also the idea that God's presence and activity was going to be with His people in their deliverance.

Verse fifteen expanded upon the name by directly connecting YHWH and the God of the Israelite's ancestors, Abraham, Isaac, and Jacob. By making this direct connection, God was linking the promises that God had made to their ancestors, not only of the deliverance from Egypt but also the land promises made to them, to the current generation. Verses 16-17 build upon this, reminding the Israelites who this God was and the land promise He had given them. God did not simply promise deliverance from slavery; He was also going to bring forth the promise of a homeland for His people, the "land flowing with milk and honey" (3:17). The question that arises out of the text then is not why or if God will deliver His people, but how?

I Will (3:18-22)

God answers the how question in the concluding section of chapter three. God gave Moses a three-step agenda for fulfilling this in verse eighteen. First, God stated, "Then they will heed your voice". The "they" comes from verse sixteen, the elders of Israel. Thus, God guaranteed Moses that the elders and leadership of the people would follow him, which served as an answer to one of his previous objections. Once the people understood that God had sent Moses and that Moses served as God's ambassador to His people, the people would fall in line behind him.

Second, Moses was to take some of the elders and see Pharaoh. While this initially does not seem like a wild statement, one must remember the situation. Pharaoh was one of the most powerful men in the world at this point in history. Presumably, one did not simply walk into his chambers and talk to him just like today, one would not simply walk into the White House or the Kremlin. How, then, was Moses going to do this? While the text is unclear, perhaps Moses' previous time as a Prince of Egypt played a role in this. If he was known still by some in the palace, that could be how he arranged an audience with the Pharaoh.

God then told Moses to tell Pharaoh, "The LORD God of the Hebrews has met with us; and now, please, let us go three days' journey into the wilderness, that we may sacrifice to the LORD our God.'" (3:18). There is some debate over precisely what Moses was asking for with this request. Many see this as simply a tiny request that God already knew Pharaoh would reject before moving on to a more detailed request of complete deliverance. Kaiser writes, "God deliberately grades his requests of Pharaoh from easier (a three-day journey with an understood obligation to return) to more difficult (the total release of the slaves) to give Pharaoh every possible aid in making an admittedly most difficult political and economic decision."[67] Thus, this initial request was not for complete deliverance but a short reprieve from oppression to worship God.

On the other hand, Stuart argues that this initial request was far more than a short reprieve. He writes

> "Three-day journey" was an idiom in the ancient world for "a major trip with formal consequences." Pharaoh would have heard it that way and would also have heard it as meaning "We want to leave Egypt for however long we choose." Moreover, the demand for the people to "offer sacrifices to the LORD our God" was yet another way of

implying—without quite saying so in so many words—that the people would leave Egypt since, as develops later in the actual event (10:25–26) the Israelites expected to worship Yahweh far from Egypt at Mount Sinai, completely out of and free from any Egyptian oversight, having taken all their possessions with them. Pharaoh's continuing resistance to the demands of Yahweh must be read in this light.[68]

Hence, Stuart argues that Pharaoh was wise to understand that this was not a short stay but was, instead, from the very beginning, a call for complete deliverance.

Either way, verse nineteen makes it clear that God knew Pharaoh's response before the request was even asked; he would not let the Israelites go for any duration of time. Verse twenty then makes a shocking but simple prediction, "So I will stretch out My hand and strike Egypt with all My wonders which I will do in its midst; and after that he will let you go." In this verse, God predicts the coming multitude of plagues that will befall Egypt for much of the first half of the Book of Exodus. Stuart writes, "God did not yet reveal to Moses how many plagues and of what sort he would employ, but there would be a variety, and they would be impressively destructive. Divinely unleashed plagues, not any human persuasion, would cause Pharaoh to let the people go."[69]

The idea of the Pharaoh not relenting "even by a mighty hand" and then God "stretching out His hand" in judgment plays a significant role in Egyptian thought. Alexander writes, "The emphasis given to YHWH's strong hand in Exodus takes on special significance when viewed in the light of the Egyptian concept of Pharaoh as a divine warrior. Typically, the early fifteenth-century Pharaoh Thutmose II is described as the "Great of Power, Might of Arm." By extending his victorious arm, God showed his superiority over Pharaoh and the gods of Egypt."[70] Indeed, many see the plagues of Egypt as directly opposed to many Egyptian gods, showing God's superiority over the Egyptian gods. As a result of these coming plagues and devastation, Pharaoh would eventually relent and let the Israelites go free.

The chapter ends with verses 21-22 describing that Israel would not go free empty-handed. Instead, God would allow them to plunder Egypt not through warfare but through divine favor. Wright connects this back to Genesis 15:14.[71] These treasures will serve two key roles for Israel. First, it would give a new nation that has been in slavery for hundreds of years some significant wealth and resources. One could even call it backpay for the servitude that they had gone through. Second, the Israelites would use some of the resources to construct the Tabernacle and the Ark of the Covenant. However, they would also use some of the resources to make the golden calf on Mount Sinai. Thus, even though God gave the Israelites resources and blessings, they could use those blessings to turn away from God in the future.

Chapter four continued this conversation between Moses and God, and then chapters 5-20 ultimately saw the completion and fulfillment of God's deliverance of the nation out of the Exodus.

Theological Implications

The first theological implication in this passage is that God's covenantal promises are undeniable. When we open up the story of Exodus, it seems so distant from the promises of Abraham, Isaac, and Jacob. The Israelites, who had been so successful through the end of Genesis, are now in slavery. It almost seems like the promises of God have somehow failed or that God has forgotten about His people. However, the story of the burning bush shows that God never forgot about His promises. He never abandoned His people. When God makes a promise or establishes a covenant, the receiver can take that to the bank. God is faithful and will never forget or be unable to come through.

The second theological implication we see in the passage is the power of God. Not only does God show His power through the miracle of the burning bush, but He also shows His power through the plagues of Egypt. His power is unmatched throughout history. Even the so-called "gods of Egypt," viewed as the most potent deities in the world during the time of Moses, were utterly powerless in the face of the Mighty God. His power is unmatched in the universe, and when He "stretches out His hand," nothing can stand against Him. He came down to deliver His people, and He did so with the power of the One True God.

The final theological implication we see in the passage is the idea of the deliverance of the Exodus. The Exodus event becomes a hallmark story of deliverance for the Jewish people. Indeed, the Passover event itself comes right out of the Exodus story. The Exodus is the ultimate example of God's deliverance in the Old Testament. It becomes a motif throughout the rest of the Bible. After the exile, the prophets look forward to a return from exile and speak of it in terms that are reminiscent of a Second Exodus. Even in the New Testament, Jesus typologically fulfills this New Exodus motif when He goes to Egypt as a child and then comes back out. That is why Matthew cites Hosea 11:1, which in its original context was a recounting of the original Exodus, as being fulfilled in New Exodus-type language (Matthew 2:15). Thus, before the cross, the Exodus served as the visible physical and spiritual deliverance of God's people from captivity.

Application

Two areas of application stand out when reading this passage. First, the Israelites cried out to God for deliverance when they were in captivity and enslavement. God heard their cries and came and delivered them from their situation. As believers, we also run into hard circumstances throughout our life.

When we run into these challenging times, sometimes we try to figure things out ourselves instead of crying out to God for deliverance. Our first response should always be to cry out to God in times of trouble.

Finally, we see in the calling of Moses some unique principles of when God calls believers to accomplish His tasks. First, before God called Moses to do anything, He prepared him in advance. God worked to spare Moses from certain death at his birth. He was then brought up in the palace of Egypt, learning from the wisest people in the world. He trained on how to write and interact in the court, tools that would help first with interacting with the Pharaoh and later in the compilation of the Pentateuch. Then, he learned about patience and shepherding in Midian. By the time of the burning bush incident, God had been training Moses for eighty years in everything he would need to become the deliverer of Israel. This story reminds us of a key idea: God calls the equipped, and He equips the called. He never calls someone to do something without preparing and equipping them to accomplish His purpose.

Conclusion

I know you have been waiting on pins and needles to hear about what happened to my brother and me with the video game. That night at dinner, my brother and I must have looked down in the dumps because my parents immediately asked us what was wrong. We explained that we had wasted fifty bucks because the game did not work, and they would not take it back since we had opened it. After dinner, my dad said, "Give me the game and the receipt," and left. He was gone for about an hour and returned with a brand-new game that worked that night. I do not know what my dad did at the store and what he said to get them to return the game and exchange it, but he was truly our deliverer that night.

In the same way, Israel needed a deliverer. They were in much worse shape than having a bad video game disk. They had been in slavery for hundreds of years. Just like a loving father coming down to save his children in distress, God came down to deliver His people. He did it through both the person of Moses and His divine power, bringing judgment on Egypt and deliverance for Israel.

Chapter Four

Mount Carmel: Power

Fire of the Lord fell 1 Kings 18:38

One of my favorite movies is Miracle, which came out in 2004. It tells the story of the 1980 US Olympic ice hockey team that defeated the Soviet Union team at Lake Placid. It was the ultimate underdog story. The Soviets had won four straight gold medals in hockey and had created what looked to be an unstoppable juggernaut. During that stretch, they had gone 27–1–1 (wins-losses-ties) and outscored their opponents 175–44. They had some of the greatest professional players in the world and had even defeated the NHL All-Star team, a team made up of players from both the US and Canada, several times.

The United States team was the complete opposite. They only had one player that had played in a previous Olympics. Most of the team was college-age players, with the average age sitting at 21 years old, making it the youngest team in US Olympic history. Coach Herb Brooks, played by Kurt Russell in the movie, knew it would be a tough uphill climb but created a unique hockey system to challenge the Soviets at their own game. He also gave the team a physical training regimen to prepare them to go toe-to-toe with the Soviets.

However, right before the Olympics, the two teams played a scrimmage in Madison Square Garden, and the Soviets won 10-3. It looked like the underdog would be decimated if they played the Soviets again in the Olympics. 1 Kings 18 gives us another excellent underdog story. Elijah, the prophet of YHWH, stands up against King Ahab and his 450 prophets of Baal and defeats them through the power of YHWH. Let's dig into this fantastic passage.

Immediate Context

When we last left the Israelites, they were on their way out of slavery and oppression with the Exodus. However, when we pick up the story in 1 Kings 18, so much has happened since that great act of God's deliverance. God came through, just as He had promised, and delivered the nation. With God's help, the Israelites conquered the Promised Land after a 40-year hiatus in the wilderness. Once they got to the Promised Land, the people struggled to hold on to their territory and God through the Book of Judges and 1 Samuel. David and Solomon briefly solved these problems, but disaster struck again with the splitting of the kingdom under Rehoboam, Solomon's son.

The southern kingdom, Judah, maintained both the Temple and the Davidic line. They struggled to remain faithful to God, going back and forth between Godly kings like Hezekiah and Josiah and ungodly kings like Ahaz and Manasseh. The northern kingdom, identified in the text as Israel, immediately went into apostasy. King Jeroboam, the first king of Israel, decided that he did not want his people going south to worship at the Temple, so he built two golden calves as counter-worship sites in the north (1 Kings 12). This change ultimately led Israel into apostasy, as not even one of their kings followed God.

In 874 BC, Omri, one of the north's strongest but most evil kings, passed away. His son Ahab took over the throne (1 Kings 16:29). The author of Kings clarifies that Ahab immediately became even worse than his father. He committed two significant sins that would ultimately impact his reign. First, the text states, "he took as wife Jezebel the daughter of Ethbaal, king of the Sidonians" (16:31). Thus, he married a gentile pagan wife, something forbidden in the Mosaic Law. Second, because of or in combination with this marriage, he "went and served Baal and worshiped him. Then he set up an altar for Baal in the temple of Baal, which he had built in Samaria. And Ahab made a wooden image" (16:31–33). Ahab, therefore, was trying to move Israel further into apostasy through direct Baal worship.

God counters Ahab's move by sending Elijah to confront the king and attempt to drive the nation back to correct worship. In 1 Kings 17:1, Elijah, the Tishbite of the inhabitants of Gilead, is quickly introduced and is given a message from God to Ahab that there will be a drought for three years. After delivering the message, God told Elijah to flee from the presence of Ahab, presumably to avoid Ahab and Jezebelle's wrath for the drought. Hence, chapter eighteen picks up the story of Elijah hiding from Ahab during this severe drought brought on by God because of Ahab's sinful idol worship.

Obadiah's Dilemma (17:1-6)

Chapter eighteen opens with a message from God to Elijah that he was now to talk to Ahab, and once that occurred, God would stop the drought that had lasted for three years. The idea of a three-year drought looks severe in the text if one assumes that this should represent about 1,095 days of drought. However, Konkel helpfully asserts, "The third year" indicates the extent of the drought according to the prophetic word (18:1). It does not mean three full years of drought, which would have been entirely destructive. It describes a severe drought that did not end the year after it began but continues into a third year."[72] Thus, the drought did not have to last three full years; it just overlapped into three years. Regardless, it would still have been a long drought that would have devastated the Israeli economy.

The timeframe also described how long Elijah had been hiding, avoiding King Ahab and presumably anyone the king had sent to look for him. Indeed, the king would have blamed Elijah for the drought, as will be seen later in the chapter, and would have been looking for him to end the drought. That Elijah had evaded him for such a long time is impressive. However, the time for hiding/running had ended, and God was now commanding Elijah that it was time to confront Ahab. Would Elijah listen to God, or would he run, like Jonah? Verse two answers that question. The text gives no response from Elijah other than that he heard and obeyed God's instructions.

Verse three then changes venues and introduces a new character to the story in Obadiah.[73] Not much is known about this figure except for two things identified in the text. First, the text states that Obadiah "was in charge of his house." This statement is a little up for debate, but it means that Obadiah was an administrator for the king to some capacity. Second, the author tells the reader, "Now Obadiah feared the LORD greatly." At first reading, this would not seem like a big deal. However, remembering the immediate context, that Obadiah could be called someone who feared the LORD stood in great contrast to Ahab and the nation.

Verse four then identified Obadiah's actions to show his fear and love for the Lord. Jezebel, Ahab's wife and Baal worshipper, had started to eliminate prophets throughout the land of Israel. Perhaps she put forth this action to stop the drought, thinking that killing enough prophets of YHWH would eventually end the drought. More likely, she was using the drought brought forth by Elijah as an excuse to do what she wanted to do regardless: massacre any follower of YHWH in the nation that would prevent her from turning the country to complete Baal worship. Interestingly, the text asserts that Jezebel was responsible for these deaths, not Ahab. Still, Ahab's actions, already described in chapter seventeen, showed that he was not only willing to allow for this transition to Baal but also was actively working towards it.

Even though he worked alongside Ahab, Obadiah went out of his way to not only hide some of these prophets but also provide for their survival in hiding. Indeed, Lamb argues that his unique position allowed him to rescue these prophets.[74] Whether or not Ahab or Jezebel knew of Obadiah's actions is not stated directly in the text, but it seems likely that he did this in secret. Constable writes, "Whether Jezebel knew of Obadiah's commitment to the Lord is unclear, but undoubtedly he and the queen were not close friends…Obviously there were many in Israel (cf. 19:18) and probably also in Judah at that time who believed in the Lord, though Israel as a whole had apostatized."[75] Hence, while Elijah was the only person who may have openly opposed Ahab and Jezebel, many in the nation secretly opposed this Baal agenda.

Verses five and six expand upon Obadiah's role and location. The drought continued, and Ahab desperately needed pasture to feed his animals. Thus, he and Obadiah went searching for the required grassland. Eventually, they split up to cover more ground in search of these resources. House argues that this whole story puts Obadiah in a unique and challenging position. He writes, "He desires to serve the Lord, yet must serve Ahab as well. Ahab sends him to find pasture during the worsening drought, yet Obadiah may know that the king is the reason the drought has come. He is a man who has tried to live his life in two worlds, and he may not be able to do so much longer."[76] Similarly, Konkel says that while Ahab is worried about a physical drought, Obadiah is probably more concerned about the nation's spiritual drought.[77] The division not only represents a spiritual divide between Ahab and Obadiah but also allows Obadiah to separate from Ahab in preparation for his upcoming meeting with Elijah.

Meeting With a Prophet (18:7-16)

Verse seven picks up with Obadiah looking for grass for the animals when he suddenly meets Elijah. The text says that Obadiah recognized him but does not say how. As Patterson argues, he perhaps recognized him based on his unique attire.[78] Indeed, later in 2 Kings 1:8, King Ahaziah knew Elijah based solely on his described appearance. On the other hand, it is possible that Obadiah recognized him based on his earlier interaction with Ahab from chapter seventeen, especially since he worked for the king and could have easily been present for the decree of the coming drought.

Regardless of how he recognized Elijah, he showed him signs of respect as a true prophet of YHWH. He first falls on his face as a sign of humility. He then calls Elijah lord in a sign of respect for his position and authority as a prophet of YHWH. Elijah was probably not used to seeing this faith and humility in Israel. If only Ahab had shown such respect and humility for YHWH, the nation could have returned to true faith. In verse eight, Elijah confirmed his mission from God by telling Obadiah to get Ahab for their meeting set forth by God.

Verses 9-12 show the unique situation that Obadiah found himself in regarding Elijah and Ahab. When he heard that Elijah wanted to see Ahab, it was not the message that he wanted to hear. He described how Ahab had sent out envoys throughout Israel and many nations looking for Elijah. Indeed, it had been years since the beginning of the drought, and Ahab believed that Elijah was the only one who could stop the drought. The fact that Ahab only sought Elijah instead of YHWH Himself shows how far away he was from YHWH.

Obadiah then makes a somewhat strange statement, saying that if he leaves to tell Ahab that Elijah wants to speak, Elijah may be taken away by the Spirit of God and not be found. Ahab would then execute Obadiah for lying about the location of Elijah and his desire to meet. Why Obadiah believes this about the Holy Spirit moving Elijah is not clear in the text, but perhaps that is how Elijah had escaped Ahab's presence throughout the years. 2 Kings 2:16 has a similar statement made about Elijah. There is other biblical precedent, such as Philip in Acts 8.

Obadiah then explained to Elijah that he was a follower of YHWH and had protected other prophets from Jezebel. Therefore, Elijah should not betray him to Ahab since he was a righteous man. Elijah assured him that he would meet with Ahab and gave him an oath to the Lord of Hosts that he would not betray him. As a result, by the end of verse sixteen, Obadiah had fetched Ahab from his search and brought him to the long-awaited meeting with Elijah.

You are the Troublemaker (18:17-19)

The difference between Ahab's initial reaction to seeing Elijah in verse seventeen and Obadiah's earlier response could not be more striking. Obadiah bowed with humility and understood his place compared to an ambassador of YHWH. Ahab immediately called Elijah out as a "troubler of Israel." Patterson notes, "Indirectly, at least, Ahab feels that the famine has been all Elijah's fault; because of Elijah's hostile attitude, Baal has been angered and so has withheld rain for the past three years."[79] Wiseman similarly states, "This was a crime against the state worthy of death, like that of Achan in Joshua 6-7 and Jonathan in 1 Samuel 14."[80] It does not even cross his mind that his unfaithfulness is the issue. Elijah is the source of the drought; therefore, Elijah must be the troublemaker who has caused so much damage to the nation. What Ahab perhaps did not think about was that if Elijah, who was not a follower of Baal, did have the power to bring drought, then Baal, the storm god, was not god.[81] Thus, the drought itself should have been the first sign to Ahab of the weakness and frailty of Baal in comparison to the greatness of YHWH.

Elijah then turns the tables on Ahab and argues that he and his predecessors are the reason for God's judgment, not Elijah. He tells Ahab, "You and your father's house have, in that you have forsaken the commandments of the Lord and have followed the Baals" (18:18). Thus, Elijah replies that Israel's trouble is not the dearth of rain but lack of faithfulness to God's covenant.[82] It is unclear in the text if "your father's house" refers only to Ahab's physical ancestors or to the entire kingly line of Israel. Ahab was not a descendant of Jeroboam, the founder of the northern kingdom, but Jeroboam had established idolatry in the nation from its very beginning. However, Baal worship had challenged the people since the time of Moses (Numbers 25).

Omri, Ahab's father, created a new dynasty when he became king but kept up with the idolatry of the previous kings. Ahab continued in this sin, and the author of Kings specifically identifies Baal worship as being incorporated into the nation with his marriage to Jezebel. Not only did he promote Baal worship, but he also actually built a temple for Baal in Samaria and built an image for the Temple (16:32). He had completely abandoned any thought of following the Mosaic Covenant and had no relationship at all with YHWH. Verse nineteen even identified that Ahab had been providing provisions for the prophets of both Baal and Asherah. Thus, Ahab himself was the only person who could be held responsible for the Baal worship in the nation and the drought judgment brought on by YHWH.

Elijah then dropped a challenge to Ahab. Ahab was to gather the 450 prophets of Baal and the 400 prophets of Asherah he was providing for and bring them to Mount Carmel alongside the nation of Israel so that the people could see the challenge. Maier III makes an interesting point concerning Ahab and Elijah's thought processes. He writes,

> Ahab perhaps thought that the prophet of Yahweh was walking into a trap, but in reality, Elijah was setting a trap for the prophets of Baal...He knew that they would be revealed as false prophets; that he would be proven a genuine prophet of the one, true God, Yahweh; and that after and because, Yahweh would demonstrate that he was "the God." The false prophets could be seized and executed. In this way, Elijah would strike a devastating blow against Baalism and against the chief advocate and promoter of this religion.[83]

Thus, Elijah, completely outnumbered by the false prophets and running as a fugitive from Ahab and Jezebel, saw one opportunity to even the odds. Ahab walked directly into the trap.

Wake Him Up (18:20-29)

Verse twenty sets the stage for the ultimate showdown between Elijah and the prophets of Baal and, more importantly, YHWH and Baal himself. Ahab gathered the people and the prophets onto Mount Carmel just as Elijah had ordered. Konkel notes, "The choice of Mount Carmel is significant as the center for the worship of a local deity that functioned as Canaanite Baal. Its proximity to the Phoenician border places the challenge to Jezebel right at her doorstep."[84] It was also a geographically prominent location and a fit setting for Elijah's contest, as many people in the nation could come and see the challenge.[85] Thus, in modern terms, Elijah played on Baal's home court. The text is unclear whether only the prophets of Baal answered the call or if the prophets of Asherah also joined. The prophets of Baal are the only ones specifically mentioned in the text, so they likely were the only ones who came for the challenge.

Elijah then challenged the people directly about their worship practices, "How long will you falter between two opinions? If the LORD is God, follow Him; but if Baal, follow him." (18:21). One cannot help but note the similar language to Joshua 24:15 when Joshua also challenged the nation to remain faithful to YHWH at the end of the conquest. Ahab had already decided by building Baal a temple, marrying Jezebel and providing for the prophets. However, the people still had a choice to return to YHWH or continue worshipping Baal. The only thing that they could not do was to continue with the religious syncretism that they had done for so long, worshipping YHWH when they needed Him and then turning to paganism the moment things looked good.

The challenge presented to the people by Elijah seems very easy to a modern reader but would not have been easy for the original audience. At this time, the Israelites were the only people in the Ancient Near East who practiced any form of monotheism, the belief in one God.[86] Every other culture around them practiced pluralism, the belief in many gods, and went back and forth in their worship between gods depending on their needs. To worship only one deity in every circumstance was unknown outside of Israel. Consequently, the people struggled with syncretism and pluralism throughout their history because it was what everyone else was doing. The response of the people was not shocking. They gave no response because they were playing the odds; if YHWH could prove He was God, then maybe the people would worship Him, but if Baal could prove he was god, they would worship him instead.

In verses 22-24, Elijah establishes the rules for the challenge. Each group, Elijah for YHWH and the 450 prophets for Baal, would prepare an altar with a bull for sacrifice. Once both sides prepared everything, each side would call upon their deity, and whoever's deity answered first with fire to consume the sacrifice would prove that they were the deity worthy of worship. The people then agreed that this seemed like a reasonable challenge.

While the challenge itself seemed simple, it was a direct assault on the power and authority of Baal. Hamilton writes, "Because Baal is the god of rain and fertility (i.e., a thunder-hurling weather god), he controls fire and lightning. So, in making the test a divine answer by fire, Elijah is taking the battle smack into Baal's turf, in which Baal is, on paper, the favorite."[87] It would be the equivalent of challenging Michael Jordan to a game of basketball or Tiger Woods to a round of golf. Elijah understood that this was an inflection point for the nation. Ahab was taking the country down a path that would only lead to destruction. The time for small challenges was over. It was do or die for YHWH worship in the nation, and Elijah would not go down without a showdown. Elijah may also have been thinking back to the stories of the Exodus when YHWH had shown His superiority to the gods of Egypt or to the events of 1 Samuel 4-6 when the Ark of the Covenant was captured and placed in the Temple of Dagon and YHWH had shown His superiority at that moment as well.

In verse twenty-five, Elijah does something incredibly shocking with the prophets of Baal. He tells the prophets that they outnumber him by so many that they should get started first. This allowance not only shows the confidence that Elijah had in YHWH but, even more so, the impotence of Baal. It would be one thing to argue that YHWH was stronger than Baal and that He could send the fire down first. It was an entirely different story to let the prophets of Baal go first. It showed that Elijah knew that Baal was nothing. He was not a true God. Baal was not even a deity. Elijah believed that Baal could not send the fire down at all. Hence, it did not matter if the prophets of Baal got a head start on him because Baal could not answer their pleas anyway.

And that is what happens beginning in verse twenty-six. The prophets prepared the bull for sacrifice and started calling out to Baal to call down the fire and consume the sacrifice. They started crying out from the morning until noon, presumably for several hours at minimum. The author of Kings makes it clear that Elijah's confidence was well placed, simply stating, "But there was no voice; no one answered" (18:26). If the prophets of Baal thought that this was going to be an easy challenge, it must have become evident quickly that Baal was letting them down. They tried dancing and leaping around the altar to get Baal's attention, but nothing happened.

After allowing the prophets of Baal several hours to cry out to Baal, Elijah then took it upon himself to start to mock both the prophets and, more importantly, Baal himself. This mocking is necessary because Elijah was not simply trying to show YHWH's power but also Baal's weakness to the crowd. He tells them to cry louder because Baal cannot hear them. Elijah then offers four possibilities for why Baal has not answered yet. First, he says Baal was probably in meditation or deep thought. Then, he says he may be busy, which many scholars view as a euphemism for using the restroom.[88] Perhaps he was on a journey and not in his usual location. Or, finally, maybe he was asleep and needed to wake up. All these potential reasons show one thing: Elijah is arguing that Baal is more like a man than God and, therefore, is not going to send the fire down and is not worthy of worship. By attacking Baal and the prophets sarcastically, Elijah was probably hoping to show the audience the sheer stupidity it was to worship Baal as a deity.

Verses 28-29 show the sheer panic of the prophets as they both hear Elijah's attack and see the lack of intervention by Baal. They began to cut themselves and work into a prophetic frenzy to get Baal's attention. Konkel describes these as standard religious rituals: "The customary gashing with knives and blades may be part of a blood ritual seeking the first rainfall. Blood letting was a rite of imitative magic to prompt a release of vital rain. Ecstatic prophesying may be a frenzied activity indistinguishable from mad behavior (cf. 1 Sam. 19:24). These rituals would take place at a fall festival for the Baal cult in anticipation of the early rains."[89] They do everything possible to get Baal's attention, but to no avail. "But there was no voice; no one answered, no one paid attention" (18:29).

A Simple Request (18:30-39)

In verse thirty, Elijah finally decides that he has had enough of waiting on Baal and that it is time to make his move. He called the people together and set up his altar for the demonstration. He then set up twelve stones around the altar, representing the twelve tribes of Israel. It is reminiscent of Joshua 3 when the people set up twelve stones after crossing the Jordan River. Elijah was trying to remind the people that even though the kingdom had split and Israel was without the Temple and the Davidic line, YHWH had not abandoned the northern kingdom even though they had abandoned Him.

After preparing the altar, Elijah did a shocking thing; he asked the people to pour water over the altar not once but three different times. This action is surprising for two reasons. First, by soaking the altar to the point that the water filled the trench, he eliminated any possible natural phenomena to start the fire. Second, the people have been in a drought for years, so the water was presumably minimal. Elijah is using one of Ahab's prized possessions to make the sacrifice to YHWH. Elijah knows the drought will end after this event, but Ahab does not, which would have been an enormous cost to him.

Verses 36-37 show Elijah's counter to the actions of the prophets of Baal. They were screaming, cutting themselves, and building up an ecstatic frenzy to try to get Baal's actions, to no avail. Elijah did not have to do anything like that. Instead, he offers a simple prayer of request for YHWH's action. He begins the prayer by calling back to the patriarchs of the nation, Abraham, Isaac, and Israel. Usually, the name Jacob occurs in this context in place of Israel, but Elijah may have used Israel to remind the nation of their namesake. He then reminds the people that YHWH was the God of Israel, even if the country had forgotten it, and that Elijah was serving on His behalf. Elijah had dedicated his entire life to serving as the prophet of YHWH, even putting his own life on the line.

Elijah then states, "Hear me, that this people may know that You are the LORD God and that You have turned their hearts back to You again" (18:37). This is the entire crux of this event. Elijah was not doing this to make the prophets of Baal look foolish. He also did this to show the people that YHWH was the one true God worthy of worship. The people had turned their hearts away from YHWH with their idol worship, but Elijah was hoping that through this demonstration of YHWH's power, the people would turn their hearts back to YHWH in repentance. Thus, Elijah's request is simple; he wants God to come down in power to show the nation that He alone is God.

If Elijah had hoped that God would come down in power, he would not have been disappointed. God came down in power with fire and not only burnt up the sacrifice but everything around it as well, including the water that had been poured out (18:38). The whole event occurred directly after Elijah's prayer, again showing the contrast between Elijah and YHWH and the prophets of Baal. They shouted for hours for nothing. Elijah prayed once, and YHWH brought the fire. What was the fire? Some argue that it was lightning, which is possible. The text is unclear, but regardless of whether the fire was natural or supernatural, the location and timing of the event, at the very least, showed that YHWH had power over nature, the same power that Baal had falsely claimed to have.

The people's response to the sacrifice's destruction completely differed from their previous interaction. Before, they had been timid about deciding which deity they would follow. After seeing YHWH's power portrayed in the fire falling, they immediately fell on their face and declared that YHWH was the true God. Walter Brueggemann sums it up nicely: "The response is decisive. The people drew the only conclusion that could be drawn...The verdict is inescapable. There are no more "two opinions." There is one opinion. Yahweh is acknowledged, Baal is routed and eliminated from consideration."[90]

However, Elijah knew that while people were willing to worship YHWH after the miracle, if the prophets of Baal were allowed to remain in the nation, they would probably drive the people back to Baal worship. Therefore, he jumped on the opportunity while the people were behind YHWH to execute the prophets. While this might seem very harsh to a modern reader, one must remember the Mosaic Covenant that the nation was supposed to be following. False prophets and idolatry were forbidden and were punishable with death (Deuteronomy 13). While the prophets of Baal may have been outsiders to the nation, brought in by Jezebel, they still lived in the country. They were technically working for the king and, therefore, needed to be eliminated for the nation to have any chance at turning away from idolatry. The death of the prophets signifies the victory of YHWH over Baal. YHWH coming down and destroying the altar with fire had not only proven His ability to outshine the false god but had conquered its prophets as well.

Theological Implications

While there are undoubtedly many theological implications we can draw from this passage, the primary theological emphasis in this passage is the idea of Israelite monotheism. Scholars intensely debate on whether the Israelites were genuinely monotheistic throughout their history or if they were either henotheistic, the worship of a single god while acknowledging the existence of other gods, or monolatry, the belief in the existence of many gods, but with the consistent worship of only one deity at a time. Practically, the Israelites throughout their history were a mixture of henotheism, monolatry, or even pluralism. The Israelites continuously walked away from YHWH and worshipped idols throughout their history.

However, theologically, did the Old Testament Law require monotheism, or did it allow for henotheism? Those who hold to henotheism will argue that Exodus 20:3 only states, "You shall have no other gods before Me," which would allow for the belief in other gods, but Israel was only to worship YHWH. Nevertheless, many other passages in the Old Testament point expressly to monotheism, such as Isaiah 40-48. The Old Testament also presents the idea in other passages, specifically in Deuteronomy 32:17 and Psalm 106:37, which argues that the pagan gods were not deities but were demonic forces. As a result, it is best to understand that Judaism was always monotheistic, even if the people did not live up to this expectation, but did allow for spiritual beings like demons to be behind the scenes of the pagan gods.

Application

This passage is one of the most applicable passages in all of the Old Testament. One of the key applicational aspects of this chapter is the importance of leadership. While Ahab received his kingship through his birthright from his father Omri, God ultimately allowed him to be king. He completely failed at this position because of his sinful rebellion and pagan idolatry. Not only did he fail, but he also brought his nation even further into idolatry by making a temple for Baal and promoting Baal worship by providing for pagan prophets. Leadership is a fundamental responsibility given by God. Not only can leaders destroy their own lives with their sins, but they can lead their people astray if they fail to follow God with all their heart, soul, mind, and strength.

A second key applicational note from the passage is that big spiritual highs only last for so long if they are not backed up with continuous righteous living. The people at this momentous event had an incredible spiritual high moment. They started not knowing who the true God was and ended the event on their faces, declaring the glory of God. This moment would have left a spiritual mark on this audience, impacting them for the rest of their lives. Indeed, they had seen the power of YHWH directly move in their lives in a manner few have seen throughout salvation history.

Nevertheless, this miraculous moment did not significantly impact the nation as a whole. While it is possible that some people had a religious moment that brought them back to YHWH, the country felt little positive spiritual impact from this event. The nation continued downward for another 150 years until Assyria destroyed it in 722 BC. They never had a Godly king. The country never experienced a spiritual revival even though they were graced with both Elijah and Elisha as prophets, not to mention several other prophets. Ultimately, while a single spiritual high moment can be incredibly beneficial in life, if it is not followed with consistent, continuous righteous living, then the momentum from the event will eventually pass, and a return to sinful living will ultimately occur.

The final note of application in the passage is the idea of standing firm in faith even in times of adversity. We see this from two different perspectives in the passage. First, Obadiah stood firm in faith and protected the prophets even when it would have alienated him from his boss, King Ahab, and especially Jezebel. Had they found out about his actions, his very life may have been put in danger. Obadiah stood firm and protected the people of God during a time of great adversity in the nation.

Second, Elijah illustrates this throughout the chapter. He was unafraid to confront Ahab in the passage even though Ahab could have quickly executed him. Elijah went up against 450 prophets of Baal all by himself. He was utterly unafraid and had ultimate confidence both that Baal was a false god and that YHWH was going to come through. Standing firm for the Lord through adversity, even alone, is the ultimate test for the believer. It also reminds us that the spiritual walk is a life of highs and lows as Elijah, so strong in this chapter, immediately flees for his life in the next chapter when Jezebel threatens it. When God comes down in power, nothing can stand in His way!

Conclusion

The young United States team limped into the Olympics after being destroyed in their last scrimmage against the Soviets. But then things started to change. In their first game against Sweden, a heavy favorite, they pulled out a 2-2 tie with a dramatic goal in the game's final seconds. They then beat Czechoslovakia, the number two ranked team after the Soviets, 7-3. Three more wins, and suddenly, the young kids were moving on to the Medal round. The only problem was that they were going up against the Soviet team that had decimated them only a few weeks before.

No one truly believed that the US team could defeat the Soviets. No one except for Coach Herb Brooks because he had been molding this young team and preparing them for this moment for over a year. They had played 61 exhibition games in 5 months before the Olympics. Brooks had worked them to the bone as much as possible to prepare them for this moment. In the movie, Kurt Russell gives one of the greatest pregame speeches in movie history. It was their time to win the game. And that is what they did. They played the game of their lives and defeated the mighty Soviets 4-3. Al Michaels, the great broadcaster, made the famous call at the end of the game. He yelled, "11 seconds, you've got 10 seconds, the countdown going on right now! Morrow, up to Silk! Five seconds left in the game! Do you believe in miracles? YES!" The US would go on to defeat Finland 4-2 to finish one of the greatest underdog stories in modern history.

While no one gave the US team a chance, there will be times when no one gives us a chance. When God calls us to do something, and it seems impossible. It looks like there is no human way to achieve God's plans and purpose. However, at these moments, God will come down in power and change our circumstances. He probably will not send fire down from the sky like He did for Elijah, but God's power has not faded, and God will come down and intervene in our lives with great power when we are faithful to Him.

Chapter Five

Hezekiah: Healing

I have heard your prayer, I have seen your tears Isaiah 38:5

Sickness, unfortunately, is a part of the fallen world. There is not a person on the planet who has not either dealt with a medical issue or had a family member, close friend, or mentor deal with a health issue. In the Spring of 2008, my mentor, Dr. Ed Hindson, a professor at Liberty University at the time, had one of these medical situations. He had a major heart attack that put him in the hospital. While he was in the hospital, he contracted a staph infection. Between the heart issue and then the staph infection on top of it, he was in bad shape.

The Liberty community rallied around Dr. Hindson and entered an intense prayer time for him. My wife had been in his class that semester, and the professor who filled in for him would lead the class in intercessory prayer for Doc at the beginning of every class. Similar things occurred throughout the campus. The doctors were doing everything that they could, but as days turned to months, it seemed as if it was unlikely that Doc would ever recover, or if he did, he would never be the same person that he was before the hospital stay.

There are many stories throughout the Bible about healing, but few are quite as intricate or essential as the healing of Hezekiah in Isaiah chapter thirty-eight. It tells the story of a king, bedridden with sickness to the point of death, who cries out for deliverance from God and is healed in perhaps a non-miraculous manner. However, it is apparent that God has His fingerprints throughout the story, and He is responsible for Hezekiah's recovery. When Hezekiah cried out for healing, God came down to meet him.

Immediate Context

About another 100-150 years have now passed from the time of Elijah to the time of the prophet Isaiah, who ministered from about 740 to 680 BC. While Elijah ministered to the Northern Kingdom of Israel, Isaiah ministered to the Southern Kingdom of Judah. Isaiah ministered from the year of Uzziah's death through the reigns of Jotham, Ahaz, Hezekiah, and possibly Manasseh. As such, Isaiah had an exceptionally long ministry of around 60 years and ministered under both ungodly kings, like Ahaz, and more godly kings, such as Hezekiah.

Isaiah chapters thirty-six through thirty-nine are a bit of an enigma in the book for two reasons. First, this section of the book moves away from Isaiah's sermons and proclamations to show the events of his time, only comparable to chapter seven. Second, the chapters are not in chronological order. Instead, chapter thirty-eight occurs first, then chapter thirty-nine, and finally, chapters thirty-six and thirty-seven.[91] This chronology is essential in understanding the passage but also shows that Hezekiah first learned how to pray for God to come down in his own life before he needed to pray for God to come down to save the nation, as shown in the next chapter.

Get Your House in Order (38:1)

The chapter begins quickly: "In those days, Hezekiah was sick and near death." The book does not give any immediate details about the timing of these events, but they probably occurred around 713-712 BC.[92] While the text does not detail the situation, it identifies three key issues in the passage. First, the text states that Hezekiah was sick. The sickness is severe because Hezekiah is bedridden (v. 2). The text describes a type of boil in verse twenty-one. Whether the illness was a type of skin disease or whether the boil was just a side-effect of the sickness is unknown, but it is a dangerous disease as the illness was killing Hezekiah to the point that he was near death. One must remember that Hezekiah was the king of the nation. He would have had access to the finest medical care available. However, nothing that the doctors could do was working to save Hezekiah's life.

Second, Hezekiah was a Godly king responsible for substantial spiritual reforms in Judah (2 Kings 18, 2 Chronicles 29). His death would set the kingdom back politically and spiritually, especially when Judah was coming out of the spiritual chaos of his father Ahaz and was in a dire political situation under the threat from Assyria. Assyria had destroyed the Northern Kingdom of Israel about ten years earlier. Assyria was now on the doorstep of invasion for Judah, despite Hezekiah's father's attempts at making deals with the Assyrian kings. Throughout Ancient Near Eastern history, the death of a king was a time of great turmoil. Nations subjugated under the king would tend to revolt at the news of the death, and other countries would invade when the power vacuum occurred. Indeed, losing Hezekiah during this challenging time could lead to political and spiritual destitution for the nation.

Young argues that the situation may have been even more severe as Hezekiah would not have had an heir yet to continue the Davidic dynasty. He wrote, "Furthermore, it is quite possible that Hezekiah at this time had no heir. Manasseh was twelve years old when he began to reign (2 Kings 21:1). If Hezekiah was to live yet fifteen years, and if Hezekiah's death and the termination of his reign coincided, then Manasseh would not be born for three years."[93] As a member of the Davidic dynasty, Hezekiah would have clearly understood the Davidic Covenant that Yahweh had made with his ancestors. If he were to die without an heir, the great dynasty would have ended, and the Messianic line would have been cut off. This threat was the very problem that his father had faced in chapter seven. Thus, it appears that Hezekiah will die,

Judah will be thrown into political and spiritual turmoil, and the Davidic Messianic line will be cut off, ending the Davidic Covenant.

However, things start to look up for Hezekiah in the middle of verse one, "And Isaiah the prophet, the son of Amoz, went to him." This arrival was what Hezekiah had been waiting for: a message from the Lord that would tell him that this was all a mistake. After all, he was a good and Godly king who was fixing the nation spiritually, overcoming the sinful legacy of his father. He also had no heir, and God had promised his ancestor David that his line would last forever and that the Messiah would come from their descendants. Undoubtedly, the prophet would give him the good news that this was only a temporary setback and that God would come down and heal him of this terrible disease.

But it was not to be. Instead, Isaiah told Hezekiah, "Thus says the LORD: 'Set your house in order, for you shall die and not live.'" Hezekiah was not expecting to hear this message.[94] This statement made by Isaiah shows his extraordinary courage in serving Yahweh, as Hezekiah could have taken his life by making this statement. In describing the nature of Ancient Near Eastern court prophets, Baker explains, "Professional prophets received a livelihood from the palace and were loath to jeopardize it. They and diviners could circumvent a negative pronouncement by pursuing omens until a satisfactory one appeared. Isaiah does not depend on these magical means; rather, he turns to his God, Who is not loathe confronting even kings with illness and death."[95]

The statement from God through Isaiah also left no room for recovery for Hezekiah, at least at face value. God did not tell him that he would die unless he repented of a grave sin that was in his life. Indeed, Hezekiah was a Godly king and, as far as the text states, did not have any significant unrepentant sins, such as King Saul or even his father, King Ahaz. It was the exact opposite with Hezekiah. 2 Kings 18:1-6 showed that Hezekiah followed the Lord, destroyed much of the idolatry in the nation, and "He trusted in the LORD God of Israel, so that after him was none like him among all the kings of Judah, nor who were before him" (2 Kings 18:5). After making this declaration to Hezekiah Isaiah left as he is not mentioned again until verse four when he is not present with him.

A Cry for Healing (38:2-3)

Verses two and three show Hezekiah's deep sickness and desperation upon hearing the Lord's news. First, he turned his face to the wall. McConville writes, "For a man still in his thirties, this deadly illness is untimely. His turning on his bed toward the wall may be symbolic of turning away from life (1 Kings 21:4), and his weeping suggests despair."[96] Indeed, that Hezekiah does not get on his knees, put on sackcloth and ash, or even go to the Temple shows that whatever this sickness was had impacted him physically to such an extent that all he could do was turn over in his bed. Beyond just hearing the news, this inability to even get out of bed would have led to even more significant distress and feelings of hopelessness and abandonment by God.

However, instead of wallowing in pity and despair, Hezekiah went directly to the Lord with one final prayer plea. He had no other option, but he also had not received any other possibility of healing from the message of Isaiah. John Goldingay sums up Hezekiah's action well and connects it back to other significant figures of the Old Testament, writing,

> Hezekiah knows how to respond to a threatening word from God and a threatening political crisis (vv. 2–3). Like Abraham or Moses, he asks God to have second thoughts. Prayer assumes that knowing God's will makes it possible to seek to get it changed. It also assumes that there ought to be a link between the lives we live and the destiny that unfolds for us.[97]

Others connect Hezekiah's prayer with that of Job.[98] Consequently, Hezekiah was not just doing the only thing he could do; he was also doing something already well-established in Israelite history.

The prayer itself was short and concise, simply stating, "Remember now, O LORD, I pray, how I have walked before You in truth and with a loyal heart and have done what is good in Your sight." Hezekiah's cry for mercy was based on facts, as in 2 Kings 18. He was a Godly king and had walked in the ways of the Lord. Wegner states, "Hezekiah stresses his piety in this verse, reminding God of his faithful and wholehearted devotion. His prayer contains no mark of penitence in the face of death. God's honour appears to be at stake: how could a righteous and loving God not listen to such a godly servant of his?"[99] Hezekiah did not believe that the Lord had somehow forgotten his faithfulness; he just wanted to remind the Lord of his actions in one last plea before death consumed him.

Scholars disagree over whether what Hezekiah is doing in this prayer is appropriate. For example, Motyer writes, "When the Lord replied (5), he only alluded to the fact of prayer and the evidence of tears; he did not comment on Hezekiah's mistaken reliance on his claim to steadfastness in action (walked ... faithfully) and inner integrity (wholehearted devotion). It is a measure of the Lord's mercy that he hears prayer even when it rests on a false assumption like the bargaining power of good works."[100] Thus, Motyer argues that Hezekiah was, in one sense, trying to manipulate God into healing him based on his previous actions.

In contrast, Oswalt argues the exact opposite. He writes, "But Hezekiah's response is instructive. He does not withdraw completely, for he does not withdraw from God. Neither does he rage against God, nor does he demand that God heal him in payment for "services rendered." Rather, he simply pours out the feelings of a wounded heart to a heavenly Father. No father's heart can be unaffected by such a cry. Nor was God's."[101] It seems better to argue for option two in this instance. Hezekiah does not demand that God heal him based on his previous actions but asks God for mercy based on his faithfulness. There is no sense of obligation on God's part in the prayer as if God is required to do this because of Hezekiah's faithfulness. This prayer sounds very similar to many other prayers throughout the Old Testament, and it points out that this is an appropriate prayer from Hezekiah.

The verse ends strangely, as it states that Hezekiah wept bitterly. The weeping should not surprise the reader as Hezekiah was physically and emotionally distressed by the sickness and Isaiah's message. Nevertheless, that the Hebrew term "יָבֶךְ," translated as "bitterly" in most English bibles, is a bit surprising. Was Hezekiah bitter at the Lord because of his situation, or was he simply bitter about his predicament? The text is unclear, but based on Hezekiah's faithfulness throughout much of his life, it is better to read the bitterness as simply a reaction to his plight and not as bitterness at the Lord.

A Message from the Lord (38:4-8)

Verse four then changes from Hezekiah back to Isaiah. It is unclear about Isaiah's location when he receives this message or if he has even left Hezekiah's presence. However, the sister passage of 2 Kings 20:4 states, "before Isaiah had gone out into the middle court." Exactly when Isaiah left and how long he was away from Hezekiah is unclear. However, that he is still in the palace hints that the Lord answered this prayer quickly, maybe even in minutes. While the phrase "come down," which is the theme of this book, is not used directly in this passage as it is in many of the other chapters, the idea is present in verse five. God is "coming down" to give Isaiah this message for Hezekiah, and part of this coming down will involve a miraculous sign (vs. 7-8) as well as a healing (vs. 21-22).

The message from the Lord consists of five separate sections. First, He connected Hezekiah to David and David back to the Lord. This connection to King David, Hezekiah's physical ancestor, is key to tying this situation back to the Davidic Covenant. Edward Young writes, "Hezekiah is reminded that David is his father, and therefore, that he himself is a legitimate ruler upon the Davidic throne, an heir to the promises that God had made to David...If Hezekiah were to die without issue, the Seed of David would not be born."[102] The divine intervention that would occur is to physically heal Hezekiah and continue the entire Messianic line that had been promised hundreds of years before to King David and his descendants.

Second, the Lord said, "I have heard your prayer, I have seen your tears" (v.5). While this initially sounds trivial, it shows that Yahweh can hear and see his followers. For a deity to intervene in the world, the deity must be able to understand what is happening in the world. These abilities are what the idols lack in their inability to intervene on behalf of their followers. Because they are not God, they cannot see the needs of their people and cannot intervene on their behalf. The true God of Israel can see the needs and emotions of his people and can hear their cries of mercy and deliverance. When Hezekiah made his prayer, he may have been unsure if God was listening to his cries. God clarifies that He was listening to every word of Hezekiah's prayer.

Third, God directly answers Hezekiah's plea when He said, "Surely I will add to your days fifteen years" (v. 5). 2 Kings adds a little more information to the story, stating, "Surely I will heal you. On the third day you shall go up to the house of the LORD. And I will add to your days fifteen years" (vs. 5-6). God promised Hezekiah that He would heal Hezekiah from this sickness that had him on his deathbed. Not only would God heal him from his sickness, but God would also give Hezekiah fifteen extra years of life. Smith, similarly to Motyer, argues that this healing is not because of Hezekiah's actions but because of God's mercy alone, writing, "God's answer did not indicate that fifteen years would be added to Hezekiah's life because he was so faithful and had done so many devout works. Isaiah does not present God's response as a merited payback for the king's good deeds; it is simply and completely divine grace."[103]

Fourth, two notable events will occur during the fifteen years that God gives Hezekiah, one mentioned in the text and one not mentioned but possibly inferred. While not explicitly mentioned in the text, if the Davidic Covenant is at play, which seems to be based on the earlier comments, then one can infer that during these fifteen years, Hezekiah will have an heir that will carry on the Davidic Messianic line. This event occurred with the birth of Manasseh, who would continue the Davidic line. 2 Kings 21 says that Manasseh started his reign after the death of Hezekiah when Manasseh was twelve years old, which would signify that he was born about three years into this extra fifteen years that God had given him.

The other critical component of God's message was that He declared, "I will deliver you and this city from the hand of the king of Assyria, and I will defend this city." (v. 6). If it were around 713-712 BC as previously asserted, then this Assyrian invasion would not occur for a little over a decade in 701 BC. However, it was clear that Assyria would be a problem for Judah. During Hezekiah's father's reign, King Ahaz made a deal with Assyria to take out the Northern Kingdom of Israel in 722 BC. Assyria, the superpower of the day, would not simply stop at Israel but would eventually make their way to Judah as well.

In this context, God was making a promise and prediction that He would defend the city when the Assyrians invaded, presumably sometime in the next fifteen years.[104] While God spared Hezekiah from his death sentence, it would not be an easy road forward. He would be the king who would have to deal with the worst invasion in Judah's history up to that point, only to be surpassed later by the Babylonian invasion that led to exile. Hence, while the pronouncement for extra life was good news for Hezekiah on the verge of death, it would certainly not be a bed of roses moving forward during those additional years.

Fifth, God proclaimed He would give Hezekiah a miraculous sign to confirm the validity of this proclamation. God said, "And this is the sign to you from the LORD, that the LORD will do this thing which He has spoken: Behold, I will bring the shadow on the sundial, which has gone down with the sun on the sundial of Ahaz, ten degrees backward." So, the sun returned ten degrees on the dial by which it had gone down" (vs. 7-8).

Prophets used prophetic signs throughout the Old Testament to confirm prophecies and promises made by God. They also validated that a prophet who claimed to be the mouthpiece of God was a true prophet, as there were several false prophets in the nation.[105] Gideon famously received the sign of the golden fleece. Moses received the sign of the burning bush. The sign God gave to Hezekiah was a simple yet miraculous sign as the shadow on the sundial would turn back ten steps (v. 8). It is unclear how God completed this sign scientifically. Still, the sign declared and confirmed that everything Isaiah had spoken to Hezekiah was the very words of God and would occur as God had predicted. Consequently, Hezekiah did not have to wait to be healed or for the Assyrian invasion to occur before he could trust the legitimacy of God's message, as the miraculous sign guaranteed that the events would happen as God said they would.

The Healing of Hezekiah (38:21-22)

Up to this point, while God had said that He would heal Hezekiah from his sickness, it has yet to occur. That changed in verse twenty-one. Verses nine through twenty appear to be written after Hezekiah had recovered. It is unclear why the Book of Isaiah has the healing event after the words of Hezekiah. The book of 2 Kings has the healing before the miraculous sign but does not have Hezekiah's words, so the passage's structure is a bit different. The text states, "Now Isaiah had said, "Let them take a lump of figs, and apply it as a poultice on the boil, and he shall recover." Isaiah told Hezekiah and presumably his doctors or attendees, to take a cake of figs and apply it to Hezekiah's boil, which would allow Hezekiah to recover from his illness (v. 20).

The question then arises whether a natural herb healed Hezekiah or if God healed Hezekiah through divine intervention. However, this is a false distinction. Yahweh, through Isaiah, was the source of the information on how to heal Hezekiah. Therefore, regardless of whether the figs healed Hezekiah or Yahweh used His powers to heal him, Hezekiah was healed, and Yahweh was the source of the healing. The significance of the fig leaves is unknown, in large part because the disease itself is not apparent. Ancient documents show that doctors used figs and other herbs throughout the ancient world to help with sickness. Ultimately, using the figs does not take away from the act of divine intervention by Yahweh in the passage.

Theological Implications

This chapter contains many theological implications, but three stand out: the deliverance of the Messianic line, changed prophecy, and divine healing. The deliverance of the Messianic line plays a key role in this passage. Hezekiah's sickness was not just a threat to his own life, as it certainly was, but was, perhaps more importantly, a threat to the entire Messianic line. If Hezekiah had died from his illness before he had an heir to continue the line, then from a physical perspective, the line of Christ would have been wiped out seven hundred years before He came to earth in Bethlehem. God understood this and intervened in history to spare Hezekiah's life and continue the Messianic line. There are many occasions throughout the Bible where God had to intervene to protect His promises, and Isaiah thirty-eight is undoubtedly an example of this divine intervention.

Another theological issue in the story is whether a prophecy can be canceled or modified. When Isaiah came to Hezekiah with a message from the Lord, he declared that Hezekiah would die. There was no "unless you pray or repent" or anything. Hence, one may wonder if this is a false prophecy if it did not happen the way Isaiah initially said it would.

However, it becomes clear throughout the Old Testament that when God makes a judgment claim, it could be reversed many times if the judged party turned back to God. Jeremiah 18:7-10 lays out this concept. It states,

> The instant I speak concerning a nation and concerning a kingdom, to pluck up, to pull down, and to destroy it, if that nation against whom I have spoken turns from its evil, I will relent of the disaster that I thought to bring upon it. And the instant I speak concerning a nation and concerning a kingdom, to build and to plant it, if it does evil in My sight so that it does not obey My voice, then I will relent concerning the good with which I said I would benefit it.

The most outstanding example of this in the Old Testament is the book of Jonah, where God does not indicate any chance for repentance and yet stays His judgment when the Assyrians turn from their wickedness. God is willing to change a prophecy if the audience of the prophecy changes, either positively or negatively.

Finally, divine healing occurs throughout the chapter. Can God use medicine and still call it divine healing? It certainly is the case in this passage. God said that He would heal Hezekiah. Hezekiah was healed through some ancient medical treatment. Even if one argues that God was the one that gave the information to Isaiah to cure Hezekiah, which is probably accurate, one at least has to admit that the chapter shows that divine healing can occur through the use of medicine, medicine that God is ultimately responsible for as He created both the resources and people that used the medicine.

Application

At every church service, people ask for prayer for healing. Regardless of whether one believes that divine healing can occur today through miraculous signs, such as in the early church, most Christians worldwide believe that God still heals and that because He does, people need to pray for healing. This healing can occur in a variety of ways. Indeed, God can directly heal a person today. However, God can also use the tools of today's medical field to heal, and this does not mean that God is not involved in the healing process.

God is also the one that chooses whom He heals and whom He does not heal. God decided to heal Hezekiah in this instance, in part because of His mercy and in part because of His promises that He had made to King David. At other times throughout history, God has chosen to heal some people and has not chosen to heal others. Christians cannot know all the details of the mind of God and His reasons for action or inaction. Christians need to pray for healing, just as Hezekiah did, and let God take care of how, when, and if that healing occurs. What Christians can know for sure is that God does, at times, come down for divine healing.

Conclusion

For months, Doc was in the hospital fighting the infection. It did not look good for quite some time. However, eventually, the situation turned, and he began to recover miraculously. He spent about one hundred days in the hospital and even had to learn to walk again and build up his strength. The power of prayer worked in Doc's life. He fully recovered, something that seemed impossible only a few days before.

Doc would go on to live for another fourteen years until 2022. During that time, he wrote more books, was the general editor of a significant study Bible, continued his television broadcast every week, and became the Dean of the School of Divinity at Liberty University. All of that would not have been possible without the healing power of God. And that healing power of God came through the prayer of His saints. When God comes down for healing, sometimes it is through miraculous healing, and sometimes it is indirectly through doctors and medicine. Still, regardless, God can come down as the Great Physician.

Chapter Six

The Assyrian Invasion: Incomparability

That all the kingdoms of the earth may know that You are the LORD Isaiah 37:20

    We do not use the term incomparable very often. After all, very few things in life are genuinely incomparable. You may love a good steak from your favorite steak house and think it is the best steak in town, but the odds are you could find another steak somewhere else that is at least in the same ballpark as your favorite. You may love a specific movie and think it is the most fantastic one ever. Still, there are probably other similar movies that are at least close to that great movie. God then is unique in our lives in that He is utterly incomparable with anything else we have.

    Several stories in the Old Testament are so powerful that they almost seem to come right out of a superhero storybook. Chapters thirty-six and thirty-seven of the Book of Isaiah are some of the Bible's most dramatic and impactful chapters. They tell the story of a nation on the brink of destruction, a pagan king in charge of the world's superpower blaspheming God, a cry for deliverance from the Judean king, and the direct intervention of God to save His people. This chapter will declare that when God comes down, He does so in an incomparable way, that the pagan gods of the world stand in no comparison to the God of the universe.

Immediate Context (36:1)

    Verse one of chapter thirty-six establishes the historical situation of the story. It identified that in Hezekiah's fourteenth year of reign, 701 BC, Sennacherib, the king of Assyria, invaded Judah and conquered the fortified cities of Judah. Assyria was the strongest nation in the world, having already destroyed the Northern Kingdom of Israel about twenty years before, during the time of Hezekiah's father, Ahaz. Indeed, Isaiah established that the might of Assyria was unmatchable and that there was simply no way that Judah could militarily fight them without divine intervention. Assyria had destroyed most of their cities and their forces, and there was nothing left for Judah to do but try to hang on to Jerusalem and wait for a miracle from their God.[106]

    Critical to understanding the events of these chapters is the events of chapter thirty-eight, as we saw in the last chapter. God had already promised Hezekiah that He would defend Jerusalem from the Assyrian invasion. Hence, when the Assyrian invasion began, Hezekiah probably assumed that Judah would defeat them quickly. This quick war was not the case, as the Assyrians overwhelmed the Judean forces and captured everything but Jerusalem.

Consequently, as the story opens, Judah is on life support, and Hezekiah is wondering where God is and when He will come down and intervene on their behalf.

The Great Blasphemer (36:2-22)

Verse two establishes that Sennacherib, still at Lachish either sieging the city or just after his victory, sent an army under the command of someone identified in the text as the Rabshakeh to threaten Hezekiah and make him surrender.[107] At first, it seems strange that an advisor to the king could speak Hebrew, but it is more plausible when one understands that Assyria had previously conquered the northern kingdom. Furthermore, he was familiar with the religious beliefs of the conquered nations of Assyria; thus, he may have been a personal advisor of the king who served as a spokesperson when conquering new lands. These details would explain his knowledge and position in the military and his ability to speak for the king.

Verse four began a speech by the Rabshakeh that can be characterized as demanding, rude, and even terrorizing. Webb calls the speech a classic study of the Satanic art of sowing doubt.[108] The Rabshakeh immediately distinguished between Hezekiah and Sennacherib, refusing to call Hezekiah a king and identifying Sennacherib as the great king. He had no respect for Hezekiah or the nation of Judah and viewed them only as a minor nuisance in the way of the mighty Assyrian war machine. He then began a series of questions in rapid succession, the idea being that there was no logical answer for Hezekiah's actions.

He first questioned what Hezekiah was putting his trust in to rebel against Assyria (v. 5). It was as if he could not believe that someone would be ignorant enough to commit this deed. Verse five moved to more questions, beginning with a question on what power Hezekiah has in his nation. The Rabshakeh thought that Hezekiah's only power was in his speech and that he had no strength to back up his words. Finally, the Rabshakeh asked who Hezekiah trusted to rebel, thinking that Hezekiah must have had some unknown reason for rebellion as it did not make sense from a military or political perspective. He was unaware that God had already guaranteed protection from Assyria during the event of Hezekiah's sickness.

Beginning in verse six, the Rabshakeh attempted to attack the two possible sources of Hezekiah's political and spiritual confidence. First, he believed that Hezekiah was placing his trust in an alliance with Egypt, something that Isaiah himself had warned against (28:15). Motyer writes, "Egypt had made its one attempt to redeem its promises (28:14), and its army had been beaten at El Tekeh. The Rabshakeh had himself seen this, but his words were more far-reaching and damaging, exposing the criminal stupidity of Judah's leaders: surely, he said, they knew that anyone who ever trusted Egypt suffered for it."[109] The Rabshakeh's word picture was brilliant. It described someone trying to hold up their body weight with a broken reed, which obviously could not hold the weight. He argued that if Hezekiah had placed his trust in Egypt, he had already failed and would pay for it.

In verse seven, the Rabshakeh switched to psychological and theological warfare, arguing that Hezekiah should not trust in God because Hezekiah had angered God by removing His places of worship. The Rabshakeh had solid intelligence, knowing about many religious reforms Hezekiah had made since becoming the king. However, he also misunderstood Hezekiah's actions. God was not angry at Hezekiah for removing the high places and altars but was incredibly pleased with Hezekiah's actions. While attempting to discourage Hezekiah, he reminded him of his faithfulness to God and why God would ultimately come through and defend the nation from the Assyrian threat.

The Rabshakeh's sarcasm came through again in verse eight, mockingly wagering that even if Sennacherib gave the people two thousand horses for cavalry, they would not have enough troops to create the cavalry regiment. It was a twofold assault: two thousand horses to Assyria were like a drop in the bucket with their mighty army, but it was more than Judah could mobilize. He attacked trusting in Egypt again, declaring that Judah could not fight a single Assyrian captain and his men when they trusted Egypt for troops and weapons. Evidently, the Rabshakeh had great confidence in his military might and thought that Judah attempting to rebel, even with Egyptian help, was almost comical.

He ended this first verbal assault in verse ten by attempting to make a common Ancient Near Eastern theological argument by stating that it was God Himself who commanded Assyria to destroy Judah. Indeed, the most famous example of this occurred in the Cyrus Cylinder, when Cyrus the Persian claimed that Marduk, the Babylonian deity, had commissioned him to capture Babylon. The Rabshakeh had probably used a similar argument against other enemies of Assyria and assumed it would be the same with Judah. However, he failed to realize that God communicated with Hezekiah through Isaiah the prophet, and therefore, Hezekiah already had confidence that God was on Judah's side.[110]

Eliakim, Shebna, and Joah, Hezekiah's advisors, had heard enough to understand that, while Hezekiah may have had faith in God's ability to intervene and save, the average Judean soldier on the wall may not have that faith and therefore attempted to lessen the intimidation by asking the Rabshakeh to speak in Aramaic, a trade language that they as court officials would understand but the average Judean would not understand. However, the Rabshakeh, never willing to miss a chance for intimidation, answered with another threat, this time asserting that the only future that the soldiers had would be to eat their feces and drink their urine (v. 12). Smith argues that the Rabshakeh wanted each man on the wall to have to process what will happen in a siege when the people ran out of food and water, hoping that the intimidation would dishearten the army and cause Hezekiah to make a quick surrender.[111]

In verse thirteen, the Rabshakeh switched his audience from the three officials to the ordinary soldiers on the wall. He started by attempting to sway the soldier's loyalty to Hezekiah. Blenkinsopp asserts that this was a common practice in Assyria as they would hold the entire population of the vassal state responsible for keeping the peace and not revolting, hoping to encourage the general population to depose or assassinate their rulers if they attempted to rebel against Assyria.[112] The Rabshakeh argued that Hezekiah was deceiving his soldiers by making them think he could save them. He also conveniently omitted that Hezekiah was a king, exclusively focusing on the "great king" of Assyria. From a human standpoint, the Rabshakeh was not wrong in asserting that Hezekiah was powerless to deliver the nation. If he had stopped at that point, he may have been justified in his verbal assault.

However, the Rabshakeh crossed the line in verse fifteen when he argued that the soldiers should not trust Hezekiah's words that God would deliver the nation from the Assyrians. Attacking Hezekiah's ability to save was one thing, but questioning God's purpose and power to save His people crossed the line. Motyer points out that the Rabshakeh was well informed and must have had some knowledge of Isaiah's pronouncements to Hezekiah, which had occurred previously during his sickness. Otherwise, it would make no sense for him to focus so heavily on subverting trust in God's deliverance.[113] If the events of Hezekiah's sickness had occurred sometime prior, word may have gotten around to Assyria that a Judean prophet was declaring victory over Assyria (Isaiah 10:5-19; 38:6), especially once Assyria had already attacked most of Judah's cities and infrastructure.

Verses sixteen and seventeen served as both a warning and a temptation to compromise for the soldiers on the wall. First, the Rabshakeh warned them again not to trust Hezekiah, which also inferred not to trust Isaiah and God as well (v. 16). Second, he told them to abandon the city and the walls and to make peace with Sennacherib by surrendering to the Assyrians. Third, he offered a counter to his previous threat from verse twelve: if they stay on the wall, then they will eat their own feces and drink their own urine, but if the soldiers surrender, then they will each have their own vine, fig tree, and water source (v. 17). He was offering them a chance to return to their own homes and leave the war behind if only they would become vassals of Assyria.

Fourth, he concluded the offer with a promise of exile but framed the exile in favorable terms (v. 17). Sennacherib would take the people away, back to Assyria, but would place them in a good land that had similar resources to Judah. This treatment was standard protocol for the conquered people of Assyria, and similar circumstances had already occurred when Israel had been exiled two decades previously. Ackroyd points out that what Sennacherib was doing was taking the place of God. He writes, "If God cannot fulfill his promises, giving the people peace and a land flowing with milk and honey, grain and vineyards, at least the Hebrews can be assured that Sennacherib will do this."[114] However, Smith points out that the exile would have been brutal, and many would have died well before making it to another land. Thus, the Rabshakeh was making a terrible situation try to sound more appealing.[115]

The Rabshakeh concluded his pronouncement in verses 18-20 with another assault on the strength and power of God, asserting that God was just another deity that could not stand up to the power and supremacy of the Assyrian military might and inferring that the Assyrian gods were superior to both God and the gods of the other nations. First, he again declared that Hezekiah was attempting to mislead the country into believing that God both could and would deliver them (v. 18a). Second, he used recent military history to try to prove that God could not defend the city (v. 18b). None of the other gods of the other nations that Assyria had conquered had been able to intervene on behalf of their country, so why should God be any different?

Next, he listed some of the kingdoms that Assyria had conquered as examples of their gods' failure to intervene (v. 19). Hamath was a major Syrian city located on the Orontes River about one hundred fifty miles north of Damascus and two hundred seventy-five miles northeast of Jerusalem. Sargon II had conquered it.[116] Arpad was to the north of Hamath. Sepharvaim's location is currently unknown, but it was in a similar region to the first two cities. He concluded with the city of Samaria, the capital of the Northern Kingdom, which had fallen to Assyria two decades earlier.

He concluded his argument with a final summary of the failure of any god to stand up to Assyria (v. 20). Young summarizes his argument by stating, "Just as these gods were not present at the time when help was needed, so God also will not be present to help when Jerusalem needs that help."[117] This declaration was ultimately the crux of his argument. God was no different than the other gods of the nations; therefore, God could do nothing more than the other nations' deities. If the gods of the nations could not intervene on behalf of their people, then God would not be able to intervene on behalf of Judah. The challenge then becomes, if God were indeed the one true God and had promised that He would deliver Jerusalem from the Assyrians, then a failure to intervene and save the city would prove the Rabshakeh correct and show that God was no different than the pagan gods who could not intervene on behalf of their people.

The chapter concludes without a response on behalf of Judah as Hezekiah had explicitly instructed the three Judeans to remain silent before the Assyrian representative (v. 21). The three men did not answer the Rabshakeh but their physical actions revealed their concern (v. 22). They went back to Hezekiah to tell him the message but tore their clothes in anguish first. In

Hebrew culture, tearing one's clothes and putting on sackcloth was frequently associated with mourning and lamenting because someone had just died or was about to die. It also occurred when blaspheme occurred, which was what the Rabshakeh had stated when he demeaned God by comparing Him with the pagan gods. Hezekiah had a similar response at the beginning of chapter 37. The Judeans knew that they faced certain doom if God did not intervene on their behalf.

Hezekiah's Cry and God's Response (37:1-7)

Chapter thirty-seven began with Hezekiah's response to the threats issued by the Rabshakeh. As soon as Hezekiah heard the news from his advisors, he too tore his clothes and covered himself with sackcloth (v. 1). However, Hezekiah also knew where to go to for help in his time of desperation; he immediately went to the temple and sent the advisors to find Isaiah the prophet (v. 2). When they saw Isaiah, they delivered Hezekiah's message of great distress conveyed through a birth metaphor. Oswalt explains the birth metaphor in vivid detail, writing

> The metaphor of labor is a telling one. All too familiar to them was the breech birth, or some other complication, which caused the mother to be unable to deliver the child although she labored herself to exhaustion and death. Furthermore, once labor began there was no turning back; either the child was delivered or both mother and child died. Hezekiah sees himself in that predicament. Jerusalem *must* be delivered, but neither he nor his government nor his people has the strength to do it.[118]

Hezekiah understood the situation's seriousness and knew the kingdom was doomed without divine intervention.

Nevertheless, in verse four, Hezekiah's message changes to one of hope for divine intervention. First, he asserts that God has heard the mocking words of the Rabshakeh. He understands that if God is truly God, then He could not sit idly by while the king and his representative blaspheme. He trusts that God will intervene, both on behalf of the promises that He had made to Hezekiah and the nation and in response to the blaspheme against Him.

Second, Hezekiah asked Isaiah to pray for the remnant left in the nation. Smith points out that this term is usually negative and refers to exiles in a foreign land after the nation's destruction. However, Hezekiah used it for the people still in Jerusalem.[119] Hezekiah knew that without divine intervention, the people of the city were in for a difficult time, as a siege would lead to destruction, starvation, lack of water, and ultimately exile for those who survived.

When the officials found Isaiah and told him Hezekiah's message, Isaiah had a strong and confident twofold response from God. First, Isaiah told Hezekiah not to be afraid. God understood the predicament that Hezekiah was in and the intimidating verbiage that the Rabshakeh had used in describing Judah's future (v. 6a). It would only be natural, even if Hezekiah believed that God could deliver, for him to be distressed and afraid. Assyria had destroyed much of his kingdom. Assyria had even destroyed his strongest fortress, Lachish. The Rabshakeh had a large army with him, and more reinforcements were coming with Sennacherib. However, God reassured Hezekiah that he had no reason to fear, for God would be with him.

Second, God predicted His deliverance of the city and the fate of Sennacherib (v. 7). God would make Sennacherib hear a rumor about a coming enemy and cause him to return to his land. Once he returned to his land, Sennacherib would die. The rest of the chapter flushes out the details of how this prediction happened, but ultimately, this prediction gave Hezekiah the confidence to stand firm against Sennacherib. Interestingly, God did not mention destroying Sennacherib's army in this prediction. It is almost as if the battle would never be fought. It is possible that God was giving Sennacherib a chance to turn away his army and avoid their destruction. However, when Sennacherib ignored the warning and sent messengers again, God announced his defeat in battle.

The Deliverance of the Lord (37:14-38)

In verses eight through thirteen, Sennacherib, hearing a rumor that Tirhakah the Ethiopian was coming, sent the Rabshakeh back to Hezekiah with a similar message attacking God and calling for surrender. When Hezekiah received the letter from Sennacherib, it overwhelmed him but also caused him to return to the temple to seek God's help (v. 14). He then spread out the letter in the temple, symbolically showing that he was placing all his trust in God (v. 15). Blenkinsopp asserts that this type of action was quite common in the Ancient Near East. For example, he writes, "We have seen that the motif of the temple visit, piety towards the deity, and defeat of the tyrant also occurs in Herodotus' story about Pharaoh Sethos who, when attacked by Sennacherib, prayed to the god Ptah and received assurance of success."[120] Other kings had assuredly attempted similar actions when the Assyrians invaded their kingdom. Still, God would now have the opportunity to show that He could deliver when the other gods could not.

Verse sixteen shows that Hezekiah had a sturdy foundation in God's creative power and divine incomparability. Wildberger identified God's enthronement above the cherubim as a sign of God's kingship.[121] Cherubim-like images were scattered throughout the Ancient Near East around temples and palaces to guard these locations as protective spirits and represent the strength and power of the nation's kings and deities. Hezekiah argued that Sennacherib was not the great king, but God was the Great King of kings.

In describing Hezekiah's prayer in verse sixteen, John Watts identified three distinct aspects of Hezekiah's theology that combined to paint his picture of God. He wrote

> You are God, you alone is not a theme found for the first time in chaps. 40-48. It had appeared in the first commandment and in 2 Kings 19:15, 19. It is basic to Israel's distinct religious consciousness. To all the kingdoms of the land asserts God's total authority over all the governments involved, including Assyria. You have made the heavens and the earth: the monotheism of Israel's worship encompassed its doctrine of creation, which in turn was the basis of its doctrine of God's sovereignty over history. These three confessions lay the foundation for Hezekiah's appeal for divine intervention.[122]

Hezekiah brought out every theological truth he could muster in calling for God's deliverance. If God was indeed the Creator and the king of the universe, He could intervene on behalf of His people and defeat the forces of Assyria.

In verse seventeen, Hezekiah distinguished God from the idols. In calling for God to both hear Sennacherib's words and see the situation, Hezekiah believed that God was active and could see and hear the events of the world. Young argues that Hezekiah was not questioning God's abilities but rather pleading with God to intervene on behalf of the nation.[123] He could have thought that the other nations fell to Assyria because their idols could not hear, see, or intervene. Still, God could, and therefore, that was the primary distinction between the true God of Judah and the false pagan gods of the nations.

Verses eighteen and nineteen combine to show two connected arguments. First, Hezekiah agreed with Sennacherib's statements because they were not idle boasts (v. 18). The Assyrians had destroyed all the nations they claimed to have destroyed. Second, Hezekiah then made a theological argument to explain their destruction; the reason was the weakness of their idols (v. 19). Mankind had created the idols from wood and stone. Therefore, the idols did not hold the power to intervene on behalf of their nations. Instead, the Assyrians tossed them into the fire when they conquered the countries the idols were supposed to protect. It is not a coincidence that Isaiah made similar arguments later in the book's second half, specifically in chapters 41 and 44. Either Isaiah had already made those statements or similar statements like them, and Hezekiah had listened to the prophet's words. Hezekiah had thought through these concepts and used that theology in writing the book's second half. Regardless of where the theology originated, Hezekiah argued that the idols failed because they were powerless. Still, he trusted that God could deliver and intervene for the people because God was much greater than the idols.

Verse twenty becomes the climax of Hezekiah's prayer, adding another emphasis to the passage. Hezekiah concluded his prayer with a cry for deliverance and argued that the deliverance would prove to all the nations that

God alone was the one true God. In effect, Hezekiah used the argument presented by the Rabshakeh and then by Sennacherib in reverse. They argued that God could not deliver the nation because he was just like the other gods that they had already defeated. Hezekiah turned that argument around by declaring to Judah and the nations of the earth that God was greater than the other gods because of His deliverance from the Assyrians.[124]

Similarly to the story of Hezekiah's healing in chapter 38, he did not have to wait exceedingly long for a response from God as Isaiah received a message from God and sent a message to Hezekiah with God's response (v. 21). First, God pictured Jerusalem as a virgin daughter who brushed off the advances of an unwanted suitor (v. 22). Sennacherib wanted Jerusalem, but the city would not accept him. Second, in verses 23-25, God made it clear exactly who Sennacherib had insulted with his blaspheme. Sennacherib was not blaspheming a pagan god, but instead was blaspheming the Holy One of Israel, Isaiah's unique term for God (v. 23). Sennacherib believed that he and his gods empowering him were greater than God and that they could take the resources of the earth without intervention. The reference to Egypt ("all the streams of Egypt" v. 25) may refer to Sennacherib believing that he could defeat the coming Egyptian force under Tirkakah or may be used as an example that nothing can stop Sennacherib from reaching his ultimate goal, which was to go and conquer Egypt. What is apparent in the text is that God had noticed the terrible pride of the Assyrian monarch.

In verses 26-29, God declared that He, not Sennacherib, had allowed the Assyrians to defeat their enemies. God determined in the past that He would let the Assyrians crush their enemies. Goldingay says, "Sennacherib has forgotten who is God. His achievements have made him talk and think as if he is. He has behaved as if he could stand tall and look God in the eye…He has taken no account of the fact that his achievements were part of a broader picture whereby God's purpose was being achieved."[125] This claim was an amazing statement by God. Though outsiders viewed Him as simply a local Judean deity, He claimed authority over the most powerful nation on the planet.

God concluded his speech against Sennacherib by declaring his upcoming defeat. God first professed that He knew what Sennacherib did at every moment, including the moments when Sennacherib raged against Him (v. 28). This can be seen as a response to Hezekiah's prayer for God to see and hear what Sennacherib had said and did. Not only did God hear Sennacherib's blasphemous insults, but heard everything that Sennacherib did and spoke.
God had not sat idly by while the nation had been attacked but had seen everything and was ready to act on behalf of His people.

Verse 29 concluded God's response to Sennacherib and declared His ability to overcome the Assyrian forces. God would turn Assyria away from the city, just as if they were a horse with a bit in its mouth. Baker points out that this language and action were like Assyria's policies. He writes, "God will treat Assyria like recalcitrant animals, turning the tables on those who treated others similarly. Tukulti-Ninurta I stated metaphorically: 'with a bridle I controlled the land.' This treatment is also depicted on reliefs, showing that it was literally applied to captive people in addition to animals."[126] God argued that He would drive Assyria away just as quickly and humiliating as the Assyrians had defeated their enemies. In doing so, He was asserting His dominance over Sennacherib and the entire Assyrian empire, including their own gods.

Verses 30-32 shifted the message of God from Sennacherib back to Judah. First, God would give the nation a sign that the people would not be carried away into exile but instead would reap their harvests and plant new harvests in the coming years (v. 30). This would be an impossible task if the Assyrians were not driven away. God promised a remnant to come out of the nation, which would be the surviving citizens of Jerusalem, as well as the continuing of the Davidic dynasty through Hezekiah (v. 32). The nation would continue for another century after what looked to be certain doom with the Assyrian invasion.

Verses 33-35 conclude God's message with a final message about God's judgment on Assyria and His divine intervention for the nation. First, God proclaimed that Sennacherib not only would fail to take the city but would never even attempt to assault or siege the city (v. 33). This would have sounded impossible to the original audience if it had not come from God. Sennacherib had already destroyed most of the nation and had an army waiting outside the city in preparation for an assault and siege. At the very least, one would have expected God to declare the siege would fail, not that it would never occur.

Second, God explained the twofold reason for His deliverance of the city (v. 35). God defended the city for His own sake, which initially sounds selfish but was understood when one realized that God's integrity had been called into question by Sennacherib. Sennacherib had endlessly told lies about God's character and power. For such blatant blaspheme, God had to act and defend His city, especially after He had already promised its deliverance. A failure to protect the city would ultimately be a mark on God's trustworthiness and power. A failure to defend the city would prove that Sennacherib was correct and that Hezekiah should never have trusted God to keep his word and intervene for the city.

Also, God mentioned that He would deliver the city for the sake of David. The line of David, the Messianic line, was in danger, as Hezekiah could have been killed in an assault, and the city would have been destroyed. Smith argues that the Davidic Covenant is not questioned because it never promises the city's deliverance. If this were true, then God would not have allowed

Jerusalem to be destroyed later by the Babylonians. Giving Judah another century gave them a strong enough foundation to return from the Exile, while Israel did not.

The chapter concluded with fulfilling God's proclamation (vs. 36-38). God sent the angel of the Lord to slay the army of Assyria, and Sennacherib, after retreating, was assassinated by his two sons back in Nineveh. It is as if the victory itself was an afterthought. If God declared it, it would happen, and that is what occurred. God thus "came down" and intervened on behalf of the people and Hezekiah. When there was no military or political way to achieve victory, God alone brought them through the invasion. He protected the city as He had promised to Hezekiah about a decade earlier in chapter thirty-eight.

Theological Implication

The theological significance of these chapters is twofold: 1) God may intervene on behalf of his people, and 2) God is different than the pagan gods that surrounded Him. Chapters 36-37 present the ultimate test case for God's ability to intervene for several vital reasons. First, the challenge presented was impossible from a human standpoint to overcome, as Judah could not defend itself from the Assyrian might. Only God's intervention could save the nation. Second, because God had already promised deliverance from Assyria when He delivered Hezekiah from his sickness, God Himself made this a test case of His power to intervene. If He could not deliver the nation, He was untrustworthy and unworthy to be called the true God.

Third and most importantly, the Rabshakeh, speaking on behalf of Sennacherib, made the ability to deliver the nation a test case for deity. Young stated it well when he wrote, "The Assyrian king is perfectly willing to regard this as a contest of the gods, a warfare between God and his deities."[127] The Rabshakeh continually blasphemed God and declared that He could not save Judah and that it was deception on behalf of Hezekiah to tell the people that He could save the nation. Therefore, God intervened on behalf of the country by sending His angel to slay the army of Sennacherib. He did it without Judah's military presence, showing that God did not need his servants to carry Him to victory. Instead, He could take matters into His own hands and defeat the Assyrians. Indeed, Judah could not even attempt to take credit for the victory because the battle was never actually fought. The Rabshakeh made deliverance a necessary element of deity, and God proved that He was the true God, greater than Assyria and their idols because He was able to deliver the nation.

Another point may be seen indirectly in the speech of the Rabshakeh and God's response to it. The Rabshakeh argued that God could not deliver the city because God was like all the other gods of the different nations that had failed to intervene on behalf of their people. This blaspheme was a mistake in part because the Assyrians did not recognize a distinction between the pagan gods and God. The argument is that no king is worthy of trust other than the king of Assyria, for no king can stand against him. What is more, the nations' gods could not protect their people, so Hezekiah's God would be unable to deliver Zion as well. The Assyrians viewed all gods as similar and thought that because they had defeated the rest of the pagan gods, they could easily, comparably, defeat God.

However, the Assyrians did not understand who they were blaspheming. By God delivering the city from the Assyrians, just as He had promised years before, He proved that He was different than the gods of the other nations. The gods of the other nations failed to intervene for their people, but God intervened, destroying the Assyrian army and delivering the city. In addition, God also proved that He was greater than the Assyrian gods, as they were powerless to intervene and protect their army or to empower Sennacherib to achieve victory over Judah. In conclusion, the primary theological emphasis of this entire section of Isaiah is showing the divine incomparability of God.

Application

We live in a world where the term "God" does not automatically mean the Judeo-Christian God. The Mormons, the Muslims, the Hindus, and many others have their gods. We must decide if the Christian God is incomparable or if He is just another on a list of various gods worldwide. The Bible makes it clear that this God controls the universe, creates it, and comes down at various times to intervene on behalf of His people. He is not simply a god but is the God. When the world argues that He is not unique, just as the Rabshakeh tried, we must, as Hezekiah did, declare His greatness and that He alone is God.

Conclusion

We live in a world today that is quite different from the time of Isaiah and, in some ways, very similar. Some people claim that there is no God and that Christians are just wasting our time going to church and believing in a "fairy tale." Others argue that their god/gods are the true god and that Christians are worshipping the wrong god. What we know as Christians is that the God of the Bible is not only real but is incomparable with any other god. He has proven that repeatedly by coming down and intervening in human history. When all the different religions cry out to their gods for deliverance, no one answers. When we cry out to God for help, He comes down and intervenes on our behalf.

Chapter Seven
Bethlehem: Person

Immanuel...God with us Matthew 1:23

  Christmas movies are a distinct genre today. Some people love Christmas movies. They watch every Hallmark Christmas movie yearly, including *White Christmas, National Lampoon's Christmas, A Christmas Story,* and *A Charlie Brown Christmas.* Others hate Christmas movies and think they are sappy and uncreative. I am on the first end. While I do not watch every Christmas movie, I watch my favorites yearly.

  My favorite Christmas movie is *It's a Wonderful Life*. In the film, George Bailey is the everyman who lives in Bedford Falls and fights against the villain in the town, Old Man Potter. In many ways, George hates his life and feels trapped in his situation. He wanted to explore the world, but every time he tried to leave, something came up that kept him in Bedford Falls. On Christmas Eve, something happens, and George finds himself in an unbelievably lousy spot. At this point in the story, Heaven intervenes and sends Clarence, an angel, down to intervene in George's life. He takes George on a journey to see what Bedford Falls would have been like if he had not been present, and it was a dark place. George realizes the impact he has made and how truly special his life is. The movie ends with a remarkable reversal; for years, George saves the town, and the town returns the favor and saves George from prison. It is truly an incredible story, but it is nothing compared to the real Christmas story.

  The Christmas story of the Bible is the most famous story that has ever been told. Mary is pregnant with a child. There was no room for her at the inn. The baby is in the manger. The shepherds are in the fields. It seems like everyone knows the Christmas story to some extent, even if it is just from watching Linus tell the story in *A Charlie Brown Christmas*. God came down in human form as a baby in a manger. Let us look at this passage and see how God came down to be with us.

Immediate Context

  Much has changed since we last picked up with the Assyrian invasion in Isaiah 36-37. Beginning in 605 BC, the Babylonians under Nebuchadnezzar started their assaults on Jerusalem, first taking many of the young men of Judah, including Daniel, and some of the treasures from the Jerusalem temple. Nebuchadnezzar returned and took more prisoners around 597 BC, including the prophet Ezekiel. Finally, in about 587-586 BC, Nebuchadnezzar destroyed much of Jerusalem, including the first temple. He carried away much of the population into exile to Babylon, just as many of the prophets had predicted would occur.

During the 70 years of captivity, the Jews lived in Babylon with varying levels of success. Daniel and his friends became administrators and advisors to Nebuchadnezzar, Belshazzar, and then Darius, but they also lived through the fiery furnace and the lion's den. With the conquest of Babylon by Cyrus the Great in 539 BC, predicted in advance in Isaiah 44-45, the Jews were finally allowed to return home. They rebuilt the temple, and eventually, Nehemiah helped to rebuild much of the city. These Jews then lived through the Greek Empire, which began with the conquest of Alexander the Great, and then, eventually, the Romans took control of the region. Thus, when the story of the New Testament opens, the Romans are now the big dog on the block and control the entire area.

When Matthew opened his gospel, he began the first seventeen verses with a genealogy, going back to Abraham, continuing to King David, and ending with Joseph, the human father of Jesus, from a legal perspective. Sometimes, people ignore these genealogies while doing their bible readings, thinking of them as a waste of time or unnecessary. However, what Matthew is doing in the passage is connecting Jesus with the promises that God made to Abraham in Genesis and David in 2 Samuel 7. Thus, Matthew sees Jesus as the fulfillment of all God had promised throughout most of the Old Testament. Here, we will pick up the story of God coming down in Matthew 1:18-25.

Conceived By the Holy Spirit (1:18)

Verse eighteen begins with an introductory statement for the entire passage: "Now the birth of Jesus Christ was as follows." What is interesting about Matthew's version of the birth account is that the actual birth of Jesus doesn't get much press.[128] Matthew spends much of his time discussing the events leading up to the birth and then the wise men's visit after the birth, but he does not address the birth story itself. All our knowledge of the events of the night of Jesus' birth comes from Luke. Matthew never talks about the inn, the stable, the manger, the angels, or the shepherds. Why would Matthew leave all those details out of the story?

The first option would be that Matthew did not know all these details. However, that seems unlikely. He was one of the apostles who was with Jesus for years and was a leader in the early church. If Luke had access to these stories, Matthew certainly would have had access to at least some of that information.[129] More likely, Matthew was not as concerned about the birth story because it did not fit with his purpose for his gospel. As verses 22-23 show, Matthew was more concerned about tying the birth story to the continuation of the Old Testament story. Once he had established that connection in verses 22-23 and the location in Bethlehem in chapter two with the story of the wise men, he probably felt he did not need to address the minor details of the birth story itself. It was an afterthought to Matthew once he had established his connections to the Old Testament. Luke then, probably writing after Matthew, would have added those details to his gospel to fill in the gaps.

Matthew then lays out the specific details of the relationship between Mary and Joseph, that they were betrothed or engaged. The engagement was vastly different from their culture than in 21st-century Western culture. Osbourne writes, " The key term is μνηστευθείσης, which means a great deal more than the "engagement" today. It was legally binding (a contract signed by witnesses) and could be broken only by a writ of divorce. If the "husband" (he was considered such) were to die, the engaged woman would be considered a widow."[130] This is not simply like a modern engagement, where it can be ended at will, and the only ramifications are to tell the families and cancel some wedding arrangements. Instead, it is not something that Joseph could break easily legally, which will play a significant role in the story.

Matthew then dropped the bomb at the end of verse eighteen when he wrote, "Before they came together, she was found with child of the Holy Spirit." Matthew wants the reader to know that Joseph is not the biological father of this child. He clarifies that it is impossible for Joseph to be the father because Joseph and Mary had no physical union before Jesus' birth. While the ancient world did not have the types of scientific knowledge that modern society has, they did know how babies were made. Matthew understood the supernatural implications that he was writing and how implausible it would sound, and that most would assume that Joseph and Mary had simply made a mistake, so he wanted to make it as straightforward as possible to his audience that they did not do anything inappropriate.

When Matthew found she was "with child," it did not necessarily mean that she was trying to hide the pregnancy. Carson writes, "That Mary was "found" to be with child does not suggest a surreptitious attempt at concealment ("found out") but only that her pregnancy became obvious."[131] Wilkins expands on this idea, writing, "By the time of the narrative in Matthew, Mary is approximately four months pregnant. She has spent three months with Elizabeth, her "relative" (Luke 1:36, 56), but now returns to Nazareth, where she "was found" to be pregnant. This does not imply that Mary has attempted to conceal the pregnancy (i.e., she is "found out"), but rather that it becomes known to others, including Joseph. This pregnancy is not yet *public* knowledge because Joseph can still divorce her privately (1:19).[132] Certainly, the fact that the greater community was unaware shows that Mary and her family were concealing this in some way, or the whole town would have known very quickly. Nevertheless, it appears that Joseph finally found out about the pregnancy once she returned from the trip to Elizabeth, as it would have been impossible for her to hide it that far along from Joseph, even by just being in her presence.

If Joseph was not the father, then who was? Matthew's answer is almost unbelievable: the Holy Spirit made Mary pregnant with Jesus. The ancient world was full of myths about deities being active in sexual unions with humanity. However, they tended to be very crass, detailed, and all about the physical act.[133] Matthew's version is entirely different. It simply explains that the Holy Spirit conceived Jesus into Mary. France argues that this is in line with the role of the Spirit in the Old Testament. He writes, "The role of the Holy Spirit in Jesus' conception reflects the OT concept of the Spirit of God active in the original creation (Gen 1:2; Ps 33:6) and in the giving of life (Ps 104:30; Isa 32:15; Ezek 37:1– 14)."[134] Hence, this is not some "divine rape" or something like that, but instead an act of divine creation.[135]

Joseph's Dilemma (1:19-21)

Verse nineteen shows the dilemma that Joseph found himself in through the situation. He was legally already considered Mary's husband, so this was an act of adultery. The text is not clear what exactly Joseph knew at this time. Did Mary tell Joseph that she had been faithful to him and that God had done this? Luke 1 makes it clear that Mary knew this would happen well before Joseph. Had she told Joseph, and Joseph did not believe her? Or had she kept the source of her pregnancy hidden? The text is not definitive, but it certainly appears in the text that Joseph did not believe that Mary had not committed adultery, either because he did not know about the Holy Spirit or he did not believe it, which would have been a tall tale for him to trust based solely on Mary's words.

One must also understand the cultural differences between dating in a modern context and the marriage process in ancient Israel. In a contemporary context, the bride and groom would have dated for months or years. They would have decided to marry based on their feelings, etc. In ancient Israel, arranged marriages were the usual practice, as they still are in some parts of the world. Mary would have been approximately 13-14 years old. Joseph would probably have been around 18-20, although some think he might have been older. They would not have had much one-on-one time together, as Joseph would have been making arrangements with Mary's father for the marriage. Consequently, Joseph was in a tough spot. In his mind, he had been cheated on by his fiancé, a young girl that he probably liked and trusted to some extent but also probably did not know exceptionally well.

Matthew then describes Joseph as a just man and explains that he would secretly divorce Mary. There is some debate on exactly what the text means when it calls Joseph a "just" man. Some argue that it references Joseph's unwillingness to humiliate Mary publicly and instead show kindness to her. R.T. France claims it goes beyond that and instead focuses on Joseph's adherence to the Mosaic Law. He writes

> That Joseph was "righteous" is sometimes thought to explain his avoidance of a public scandal because he was "merciful" or "considerate," but the more fundamental sense of the word is of one

who is careful to keep the law. The law, as then understood, required the termination of the engagement in the case of "adultery;" in OT times, the penalty for adultery was stoning. Deut 22:13– 21 deals specifically with the case of a woman found not to be a virgin at the time of marriage, and 22:23– 24 with that of consenting "adultery" on the part of an engaged woman. However, divorce was the usual course in the first century (when Roman rule abolished Jewish death penalties).[136]

Hence, while Joseph was showing Mary mercy by not shaming her, he was still following the law by not marrying her based on supposed adultery. Instead of publicly shaming her and her family, he called off the wedding. Mary would probably be sent away to have the baby in secret, keeping her and her family standing in the community.

While Joseph was figuring out the details of the divorce and the implications that would come from it, God intervened by sending an angel to him in a dream. While the angel is not named, it is probably Gabriel, the messenger angel who visited Daniel and Mary. Giving messages in dreams was a common occurrence throughout the Bible. Osbourne notes, "It was common for God to send revelatory messages via dreams (Gen 28:12; 37:5–9; Num 12:6; Judg 7:13; Dan 2:3; 4:5; 7:1). Dreams are a primary form for God's sovereign control as he reveals his will and guides human actions according to his will."[137]

The angel immediately calls Joseph "son of David." In the context of the book, Matthew connects Joseph back to the lineage that Matthew had already established in the first seventeen verses of the book. Thus, Matthew connected Joseph and Jesus as his legal heir with the Davidic line. In 2 Samuel 7, God promised David his line would reign forever. After the destruction of Jerusalem and the end of the royal line in 586 BC, many Jews probably assumed that this promise had failed. Nonetheless, Matthew's connection showed that God did not forget this promise and that God would ultimately fulfill this promise with the coming of this child from the Davidic line.

The angel then told Joseph, "Do not be afraid to take to you Mary your wife" (1:20). Why would Joseph be afraid to take Mary as his wife? Wilkins argues, "The command "do not be afraid" does not imply that fear figures into Joseph's dilemma about his pregnant betrothed Mary. Rather, he is not to fear the consequences and stigma attached to him when he completes the wedding stage of the marital relationship."[138] Even if Joseph trusts Mary and understands that she did not cheat on him, it is doubtful that other people would either know that story or, even if they did, believe it. Joseph would then have to sign up for a lifetime of ridicule. He would be known as the man who married the girl who cheated on him for the rest of his life. It would take great courage to sign up for that burden.

At this point, Joseph was probably wondering why the angel would tell him to marry a woman that he believed was an adulterer. The answer is given by the angel in that Joseph is finally told the inside scoop that Mary did not cheat on him, but God was behind her pregnancy. Imagine what Joseph must have been thinking. Yes, it is good that his fiancé was faithful on the one hand. On the other hand, he would now be the human father to the literal Son of God.

Then, the angel told Joseph both this child's name and mission. First, he is to name the child Jesus, which means "Yahweh is salvation or the Lord saves."[139] Second, his mission is described as "for He will save His people from their sins." This simple line that the angel told Joseph would ultimately change the world. Carson writes, "There was much Jewish expectation of a Messiah who would "redeem" Israel from Roman tyranny and even purify his people, whether by fiat or appeal to law. But there was no expectation that the Davidic Messiah would give his own life as a ransom (Mt 20:28) to save his people from their sins."[140]

This concept explains the primary issue that Jesus constantly runs into throughout the Gospels. The people, even the disciples, were looking for a political deliverer. In contrast, Jesus came as a spiritual deliverer. For example, in Matthew 16:21-23 Jesus told the disciples that He was going to Jerusalem to die, and the disciples, mainly Peter, denied that this would/could occur. Jesus even calls the words that Peter states as coming from Satan. The disciples also argued about who would have the greatest seat in the kingdom (Mark 10:35-45). It was not until after the crucifixion in the early sermons of Acts that the apostles finally started to preach about Jesus' spiritual deliverance. Matthew clarifies that before Jesus was born, God planned for Jesus to bring spiritual deliverance from sins.

The Virgin Birth (1:22-23)

Matthew briefly interrupts Joseph's story in verses 22-23 to explain that the Old Testament had predicted this idea of Mary being pregnant as a virgin. He quotes Isaiah 7:14 from the Greek Septuagint and says it is being fulfilled. However, scholars greatly disagree with what he is doing with the passage in Isaiah 7:14. Messianic Jewish scholar Michael Rydelnik writes, "In my experience, Isa 7:14 is the most controversial of messianic prophecies."[141] A brief overview of the Isaiah 7:14 passage itself is necessary to understand its issues.

In Isaiah 7, Rezin, king of Syria, and Pekah, king of Israel, were planning to attack King Ahaz of Judah. Assyria, the superpower of their day, threatened them, and they wanted Ahaz to help them create a three-nation alliance against Assyria. Ahaz did not want to go against Assyria, so the two kings would join to kill Ahaz and put a puppet king on the throne. Ahaz was a member of the Davidic line, so this was a direct attack on the Davidic

Covenant. God sent Isaiah to the king to encourage him, but Ahaz did not want to talk to Isaiah or God. Isaiah offered to give him a sign to show God's power, but Ahaz refused to ask for a sign. At this point, verse fourteen was delivered, which states, "Therefore the Lord Himself will give you a sign: Behold, the virgin shall conceive and bear a Son and shall call His name Immanuel."

Three camps exist on this issue. The first camp argues that Isaiah 7:14 was never a messianic prophecy. Holders of this position say that the virgin in Isaiah was simply someone who lived during the time of Ahaz and was currently a virgin at the time of the prophecy. Presumably, this girl would get pregnant and would have a child. Before this child would be old enough to know wrong from right (7:16), the two enemy kings would be defeated. Thus, in this view, Matthew is simply looking for a passage in the Old Testament that would make it look like Mary's pregnancy would "fulfill" a prediction and took Isaiah 7:14 out of its original context and meaning.

A second view holds that most of the first view is correct, that there was a virgin/young girl who would get pregnant during the time of Ahaz, but that typologically, Jesus also fulfilled this passage, and that is why Matthew saw this connection. Thus, there was an initial fulfillment during the time of Isaiah and then a further messianic fulfillment with Mary. A third view argues that the woman Isaiah predicted was always Mary and that the virgin birth of Jesus was always in mind. Evangelicals hold either views two or three on this passage.

The most significant aspect of this verse in Matthew is the name Immanuel, translated as "God with us." This name gives a clear indication that this messianic child that was to be born was not simply normal. Instead, He was a divine child. Mary also heard similar statements in Luke 1 when Gabriel addressed her. Wilkins summarizes the issue well by stating, "We have no record of Jesus ever being called "Immanuel" by his family or followers. Instead, as Matthew translates it for us, we see that the name is intended as a title to indicate Jesus' messianic identity: "God with us." Both his common name and his titular name indicate profound truths: *Jesus* specifies what he does ("God saves"), and *Immanuel* specifies who he is ("God with us").[142]

One cannot miss the significance of this statement. Think of the trajectory we have seen throughout the Old Testament leading up to this passage. In the Garden of Eden, man had direct access to and communed with God. However, the fall of man in Genesis 3 led to a separation between God and humanity. A temporary solution was established in the Book of Exodus with the creation of the Tabernacle. This setup allowed God's presence to live among the people. In fact, their entire camp was set up so that the Tabernacle and the presence of God were at the center of their society. God moved in and was their neighbor. The problem was that He was not an ordinary neighbor you could walk up to and interact with daily. Only the high priest could enter the Holy of Holies and only on the Day of Atonement. God was their neighbor, but sin had still corrupted their relationship.

The temporary nature of the Tabernacle was ultimately replaced with the construction of Solomon's Temple, but the same issues persisted. Direct access to God was still not possible. Eventually, because of the sin of the people, the Babylonian invasion and exile destroyed the limited access to God through the Temple. The sins of the people continued to block access to God. While He came down at various times in the Old Testament, as we saw in the first six chapters of this book, it was always a temporary and limited thing.

Matthew 1 changes all of this. God was now with us. Jesus, God in the person, was coming down from Heaven to dwell with man again. Osbourne aptly asserts, "In fact, Jesus is the presence of God in a sense like John 1:14, in which Jesus is the incarnate Shekinah; that is, in Jesus God is once again walking planet Earth. "Shekinah" comes from the Hebrew šākan, which means "to live, dwell," and in the OT the word referred to God's actually dwelling in the Most Holy Place. It came to mean that the glory of God was dwelling on planet Earth."[143] Not only that, but He was also coming to save the people from their sins, the very thing that had destroyed their relationship with God from the beginning. The Christmas story is not just a lovely story about a baby in a manger but is a culmination of God's plan to fix the problem of Genesis 3. Jesus Himself had come down from the heavenly throne to intervene on behalf of humanity.

Joseph's Obedience (1:24-25)

Verse twenty-four picks back up with the story of Joseph. He heard from the angel in the dream that Mary had been faithful and God was working through the entire situation. Yet, Joseph still had a decision to make. Should he trust that the message he received was legitimate? Maybe he just had a weird dream brought on by the situation's stress and was hoping it was true. The text does not give us any insight into Joseph's thoughts on these issues. What it does state is the faithfulness of Joseph. He woke up and did what the Lord commanded him and married Mary. He obeyed and called his son's name Jesus, just as instructed.

Finally, Matthew mentions something extremely specific in the text, that Joseph "did not know her till she had brought forth her firstborn Son" (1:25). Carson asserts, "Both Joseph and Matthew wants to make Jesus' virginal conception quite unambiguous, for he adds that Joseph had no sexual union with Mary (lit., he did not "know" her, an OT euphemism) until she gave birth to Jesus (v.25). The "until" clause most naturally means that Mary and Joseph enjoyed normal conjugal relations after Jesus' birth. The imperfect *eginōsken* "did not know [her]," does not hint at continued celibacy after Jesus' birth but stresses the faithfulness of the celibacy until Jesus' birth."[144] No one could argue Mary's virginity until after Jesus had already been born, showing the supernatural nature of the event.

Theological Implications

The concept of the virgin birth of Jesus is one of the most attacked elements of Christianity. Critics argue that it is not scientifically possible or was just based upon ancient myths that also had an idea of their gods coming from virgin births. This objection has called some Christians to ask, does holding to the virgin birth even matter? The answer is absolutely yes! Two reasons stand out. First, if we believe in the inspiration and inerrancy of the Bible, then we cannot deny the virgin birth. Wayne Grudem writes, "Scripture clearly asserts that Jesus was conceived in the womb of his mother Mary by a miraculous work of the Holy Spirit and without a human father."[145] The virgin birth happened, or Matthew and Luke made up a story about Jesus' birth. Suppose they were willing to make up a story about some supernatural birth that did not happen. In that case, they should not be trusted for any other supernatural events they record, including the resurrection.

Second, the virgin birth plays a significant role in the deity, humanity, and sinlessness of Jesus Christ. The virgin birth made the uniting of full deity and full humanity possible in one person. This unification was how God sent his Son (John 3:16; Gal. 4:4) into the world as a man.[146] While God could have done this some other way, possibly by creating Jesus as a complete human in Heaven and sending Him to Earth, He chose not to and instead chose the virgin birth as the way to unite the deity and humanity. The virgin birth also makes Christ's true humanity possible without inherited sin.[147] The work of the Holy Spirit in creating Jesus' physical human body likely allowed Him to be in a human body without sin. Consequently, the virgin birth was necessary for God to truly come down in the person of Jesus.

We also see God's plan identified in the coming down of Immanuel. The problem of sin would be overcome with Immanuel's coming. It is through His coming that Jesus would save His people from their sins. The little baby in the manger would grow up to be the crucified Savior and the resurrected King. God's plan of redemption began in Genesis 3:15, but it really begins to come into focus with the coming of Immanuel.

Application

Perhaps the most significant application that we can see in this passage is the idea of trusting God even when it does not make sense to us. Joseph was twice put into almost impossible situations. First, he had to come to grips with his fiancé cheating on him and how to work through that without embarrassing her and her family while also staying faithful to the Mosaic Law. Then, Joseph had to come to grips with the idea that not only had Mary not cheated on him, but God had made her pregnant. Not only this, but he would have to live the rest of his life with people trying to shame him and his family based upon actions that were not only entirely outside their control but were established by God. Sometimes in our lives, God will call us to do things that do not make sense and, in our minds, might seem a little crazy. However, our response should not be to question God's ways and plans; instead, we should follow Joseph and Mary's models and obey God even when it does not make sense.

Conclusion

We began this chapter looking at the story of *It's a Wonderful Life*. In the movie, Heaven intervenes in the life of George Bailey by sending Clarence down to show him a different perspective about his life. While it is an exceptional story in the movie, the true Christmas story is much more incredible. Humanity was in a remarkably similar situation to George Bailey. While he was in a challenging problem that was leading him to prison, humanity was in a more difficult situation that was leading to Hell. Just as George could do nothing to save himself, humanity could do nothing in its own power to save itself. No matter how hard we tried, we could not restore that broken relationship with God.

In the movie, Heaven intervened on behalf of George with an angel. In the real story, God took it one step further. Instead of sending down an angel to help, God Himself came down from Heaven to help us. Instead of showing us what life would be like without us, God showed us what life could be like with Him again. God did not send a replacement when all the chips were down, but He Himself came down personally to deliver us.

Chapter Eight

Golgotha: Atonement

Come down from the cross   Matthew 27:42

Superheroes have been a popular genre for almost a century, first in comic books and then in movies and television shows. One of the greatest superheroes ever made was that of Clark Kent, aka Superman. He was an individual from the planet Krypton that came to Earth and became a superhero with incredible superpowers. He fights for "truth, justice, and the American way" and is a paradigm of virtue.

While there have been many incarnations of Superman throughout the years, my favorite is the television show *Smallville*. The show is set before Superman becomes a superhero and focuses more on Clark Kent, growing up in high school and eventually moving to Metropolis. Throughout the show, Clark constantly saves people and hides his powers from the public. Another interesting aspect of the character is that he dislikes killing his enemies. Hence, he continually holds back his powers to stop his enemies without doing too much damage to them.

The crucifixion story is again one of the Bible's most famous stories. Many are familiar with the story from Sunday School or Vacation Bible School. Others are familiar with the story from *The Passion of the Christ*. Jesus was arrested and then crucified on a Roman cross. While it is such a familiar story, sometimes we can overlook some of its details, such as the idea of Jesus coming down from Heaven but refusing to come down from the cross. Let's dig in.

Immediate Context

We last saw the baby Jesus being born in Bethlehem in Matthew 1. We know little about Jesus' childhood besides a few stories about His interactions in the Temple and His growth and development. The story then picks up with the start of Jesus' ministry. He gathered twelve disciples and went through much of the region, centered in Galilee but occasionally visiting Jerusalem. He preaches, heals, casts out demons, and controls creation. Great crowds gather and are amazed at His abilities and His words.

However, the Jewish leaders, outside of Nicodemus and Joseph of Arimathea, are not happy with the coming of Jesus. They do not accept His messianic claims but instead claim that His miracles are from the power of Satan (Matthew 12:24). Jesus consistently rebukes them for their unbelief and their hypocrisy, which infuriates them even more. They begin to plot to get rid of Jesus as soon as possible.

When Jesus arrives in Jerusalem on Palm Sunday and appears to be gaining momentum with the people as a Messianic figure, the religious leaders know they must strike quickly. They cannot allow Jesus to become a threat to them, both as a spiritual figure and as a possible threat to Rome, with whom the Sanhedrin had good relations and needed to stay in power. They get one of Jesus' disciples, Judas Iscariot, to betray Jesus and arrest Him in the Garden of Gethsemane. They beat Him and put Him through a sham trial. They then took Jesus to Pilate, who initially found Jesus innocent but eventually was pressured into allowing Jesus to be crucified. At this moment, we will pick up the story in Matthew 27.

The Lead Up to the Cross (27:27-34)

After Pilate sentenced Jesus to crucifixion, he gave Jesus to the Roman soldiers, who tortured and mocked Jesus in multiple ways. First, they scourged Jesus. Blomberg describes scourging as "often fatal, employed a metal-tipped whip known as the *flagellum*, which repeatedly ripped into the naked flesh of the victim's back."[148] This beating would have severely hurt Jesus, almost to the point of death, but it was just the beginning of His torment.

Second, in verse twenty-seven, they took Jesus to the Praetorium with the rest of the Roman soldiers. The Praetorium was the official residence of the Roman governor, but the term was also used for the camp of the troops who served him.[149] Thus, at this point, Jesus was entirely outside of the reach and power of the Jewish leaders but was also at the mercy of the Roman soldiers, who viewed Him solely as a convicted criminal. They are most likely unaware of Jesus' innocence. Indeed, they seem to honestly think that He had legitimately claimed to be the political King of the Jews. They believed that Jesus was a rebel against Rome that needed to be crushed and made an example to prevent further rebellion.

Third, because of this assumption by the Roman soldiers, they begin to mock Jesus as a fake king. They stripped Him, put a scarlet robe on Him, twisted a crown of thorns on His head, and bowed to Him, mocking Him as the King of the Jews. Leon Morris notes the irony of the situation. He writes, "Matthew is describing a highly ironical situation; the soldiers went out of their way to produce trappings of royalty as a means of ridiculing one who was to be crucified as a King, whereas he really was king in a fuller and wider sense than they had any idea of."[150] France notes that this would have been "unusually good sport, and for non-Jewish soldiers to have such an opportunity of abusing a Jewish dignitary with impunity was a chance not to be missed."[151] The Romans, for the most part, did not like the Jews, viewing them as weird and different from the other peoples under their authority. They would not worship the Roman gods and were always considered suspicious.

One cannot help but think about Isaiah 52:13-53:12 when reading this passage. Jesus completely fulfills this role of the Suffering Servant that Isaiah described. The first connection between the Suffering Servant and Jesus is this idea of being beaten. Isaiah 52:14 states, "Just as many were astonished at you, so His visage was marred more than any man, and His form more than the sons of men." Isaiah predicted that the Suffering Servant would be beaten so severely that He would almost be unrecognizable as a human being. Between the scourging and then the crown of thorns and the various beatings, Jesus would have been beaten to the point of death. Anyone who has ever watched the movie *The Passion of the Christ* understands the severe beatings that Jesus took throughout these events, even before He made it to the cross.

Isaiah 53:3 also describes the hatred and mocking that the Suffering Servant would receive. Isaiah predicted, "He is despised and rejected by men, a Man of sorrows and acquainted with grief." Jesus fits this prediction perfectly. He was first despised and rejected by the Jewish religious leaders of His day. He then was despised and mocked by the Roman soldiers throughout His beatings. The soldiers mocked Jesus' kingship and even spat on Him. They had no qualms about mocking and beating Jesus, just as Isaiah had predicted.

Verse thirty-one shows an interesting transition. Matthew writes, "And when they had mocked Him, they took the robe off Him, put His clothes on Him, and led Him away to be crucified." That the Roman soldiers did all the mocking of Jesus as King of the Jews behind the walls of the Praetorium and then changed him back to his clothes shows two things. First, they did not want the Jewish people to see them mocking a "King of the Jews" in the manner that they were mocking Him. While the Jewish religious leaders hated Jesus and were ultimately responsible for the entire situation, the average Jewish person may not have been comfortable with the hated Romans mocking a Jewish person in this manner.

Second, that they put Jesus' clothes back on Him again shows that the Romans did not want to offend the Jews. Osborne asserts, "Normally, the prisoner went naked to the place of execution. This odd departure from custom may have been done because the soldiers would not scourge him further. Or, perhaps better, they considered Jewish sensitivities against nakedness at Passover. During the feast, Pilate would not want to anger the crowds unduly."[152] The fact that Jesus kept His clothes up to the cross is significant as it fulfills a prophecy about them casting lots for His clothes.

On Jesus' way to the crucifixion site, the Roman soldiers found someone else, Simon of Cyrene, to carry Jesus' cross (27:32). While Matthew does not say why this occurred, presumably Jesus had been so severely beaten previously that He could not take it Himself. France comments,

> The condemned man would usually be made to carry his crossbeam. We are not told why Jesus was not made to do so. Still, it is a reasonable assumption that after the flogging, he was not physically capable of it. He managed it only as far as the city gate ("as they went out" probably refers to leaving the city). Using their right to commandeer local labor, the soldiers forced a bystander to carry it instead. The preservation of

Simon's name and country of origin suggests that he may subsequently have been involved with the Christian community. Still, nothing indicates that he had hitherto had anything to do with Jesus.[153]

France also argues that the passage is ironic. Simon Peter, who had claimed that he would die for Jesus (26:35), was nowhere to be found, and so a new Simon was needed to carry the cross.[154]

Eventually, they arrived at the place of the crucifixion site, called by Matthew "Golgotha, that is to say, Place of a Skull" (27:33). This location is difficult for scholars to pin down clearly. Morris notes, "The name of the place is well documented in the Gospel tradition, but with the information at our disposal we are not able to identify it with any certainty."[155] Osborne comments, "Golgotha" is the Greek transliteration of the Aramaic Gulgultā, "skull." It is not known whether the place was called that because the knoll resembled a skull or because it was the Roman site for executions...The main thing we know is that it was on the main highway coming into Jerusalem. The Romans always executed criminals on major thoroughfares as a warning to the citizens."[156]

Once they arrived, the Roman soldiers tried to get Jesus to drink a mixture of sour wine and gall, but Jesus refused to drink it. Some argue that this was meant to dull Jesus' senses, which Jesus did not want as He was willingly going to the cross. Others say that this was something that the Romans gave Him to torture Him even more, as He would have been thirsty, and yet the drink would have tasted awful. Regardless, Jesus refused to drink it either way.

The Crucifixion (27:35-44)

Ironically, Matthew spends very little time addressing the details of the crucifixion itself. Blomberg gives some details on what the crucifixion would have looked like, writing,

> So Christ is nailed to the cross (this is what is implied by "crucified" in v. 35)—his feet nailed together at his ankles at the bottom of a vertical pole, his hands nailed at the wrists to either end of the crossbeam. Crucifixion was undoubtedly one of the most gruesome forms of torture and death humans have ever invented. It involved prolonged suffering for up to several days. The final cause of death was usually asphyxiation, since the victim finally became too weak to lift his head far enough off his chest to gasp for air.[157]

The beatings that Jesus had already received would have nearly killed Him already. The crucifixion would have painfully finished the job.

Isaiah 53:7 stands out when reading through this passage. Isaiah wrote, "He was oppressed, and He was afflicted, yet He opened not His mouth; He was led as a lamb to the slaughter, and as a sheep, before its shearers are silent, so He opened not His mouth." Throughout His trial and leading up to the crucifixion, Jesus never tried to stop the trial or His punishment. Isaiah compares the Servant to the Passover Lamb being led to slaughter. Jesus could have stopped this sham at any moment, and yet He willingly went through it for humanity.

The rest of verse thirty-five is used by Matthew to connect the events of Jesus' crucifixion with another messianic prophecy from Psalm 22:18. Morris notes that "A noteworthy feature of Matthew's account is the large number of places where the language echoes Old Testament passages; they show us that Matthew sees the fulfillment of Scripture in what took place that fateful day."[158] Jesus' clothes being gambled on by the Roman guards would have meant very little to the guards as they would have been worth very little. However, Wilkins notes that "By so doing they take away his final external dignity and protection from the flies and elements that torture his beaten body."[159] Nailed to the tree and without the protection of his clothes, Jesus is both shamed and physically helpless.

The soldiers continued the mocking that they had earlier by putting up a sign over Jesus' head reading, "This is Jesus, King of the Jews." Matthew then notes that Jesus had been crucified between two robbers. Osborne notes two critical aspects to this detail: "The two criminals were undoubtedly insurrectionists like Barabbas; he was the leader, and Jesus was crucified in the central position in his place. It was virtually the only crime punishable this way. It probably alludes to Isa 53:12, "numbered with the transgressors." Ironically, the right and the left of Jesus are where James and John wished to be (20:20–23), but there is no glory.[160] Thus, Matthew twice sees Jesus take Barabbas's place, first at the trial and then on the cross.

Verses 39-44 form a unit of three different groups that mock Jesus: the passersby, the chief priests and their allies, and those crucified with Jesus.[161] While they think their mocking is justified, ultimately, every detail of the ridicule is eventually shown to be true, making the mockers unwitting evangelists.[162] The first group attacked Jesus because of His claims about the destruction of the Jewish Temple, which had been misunderstood in John 2:19. His critics used this claim against Him at the trial in Matthew 26:61. They continued the mocking by telling Jesus if He was the Son of God, then He should be able to save Himself by coming down from the cross.

The religious leaders built on this initial ridicule by adding, "He saved others; Himself He cannot save. If He is the King of Israel, let Him now come down from the cross, and we will believe Him" (27:42). Perhaps no more ironic statement has ever been made in world history. Everything that the religious leaders wanted Jesus to do was the exact opposite of the plan of God. By not saving Himself, Jesus was ultimately saving others. It was through His death and resurrection that the sins of humanity would be paid. If Jesus had saved Himself in this moment, humanity would not have been offered salvation.

They also questioned His messianic title, the King of Israel. They wanted to see a miracle of Jesus "coming down" from the cross. Only if they saw that would they believe He was the true Messiah. Their mocking and their theology were utterly in error. By asking Jesus to come down from the cross, the religious leaders were essentially continuing the temptation of Jesus from Matthew 4. Satan had tempted Jesus to use His supernatural abilities to ignore His messianic mission, and Jesus had refused. Now, the religious leaders were doing the same thing.

Interestingly, the religious leaders sought a miracle to believe in Jesus' Messianic claims. Jesus had already done literally thousands of miracles throughout His ministry, yet these same religious leaders had denied His power and authority and even accused Him of working for Satan. Even if Jesus had come down from the cross, it is unlikely that these religious leaders would have believed in Him. After all, they had already seen many miracles and would refuse to acknowledge His resurrection in just a few days.

The religious leaders take it even a step further when they claim, "He trusted in God; let Him deliver Him now if He will have Him; for He said, 'I am the Son of God'" (27:43). Essentially, what the religious leaders are saying is that God was punishing Jesus by crucifying Him and that if Jesus was indeed God or even a just person, God would have rescued Him. Thus, they trust that God is punishing this rebel who falsely claimed to be God but because God would never have allowed His son to die in such a humiliating manner.[163] It is not even a possibility in their mind that God would allow a just man to die in this manner. Isaiah 53:10 answers this: "Yet it pleased the LORD to bruise Him; He has put Him to grief." Isaiah hints that God the Father Himself is involved in this process, not because Jesus deserved this punishment but because Jesus was taking on the punishment of humanity through this.

The Death of the Son of God (27:45-50)

Verse forty-five is a challenging verse to interpret. The text states, "Now from the sixth hour until the ninth hour, there was darkness over all the land." What does the text mean when it says there was darkness over the whole land? Does it just mean that it happened to be a dark and cloudy day? Not likely. Morris argues, "We should understand the darkness as supernatural, leading up to the time when the Son of God breathed his last. It was not a local phenomenon peculiar to Jerusalem and its immediate environs, for all three Synoptists tell us that it was over all the land, the land of Israel. They mean that it was not a natural phenomenon but the result of divine intervention."[164]

God used darkness throughout the Bible to show a time of great punishment/judgment. In the Exodus, the ninth plague given to Pharaoh was a plague of darkness. Similarly, in the Book of Revelation, the fifth bowl judgment is also darkness over the kingdom of the antichrist. Why is God putting darkness over the land? Because it is at this point that Jesus was taking on the punishment for the sins of humanity. We must remember that Jesus did not just take the physical punishment of the cross, but also the wrath of God was poured out on Him (Isaiah 53:4; 1 Peter 2:24; Galatians 3:13).

After three hours of darkness, Jesus cried out, "Eli, Eli, lama sabachthani?" that is, "My God, My God, why have You forsaken Me?" (27:46). This is a direct quotation from Psalm 22:1, which is another Old Testament quotation that Matthew links to in the passage. There is some debate on what exactly Jesus meant with this quotation. Some see it as a faith statement placing trust in the God who will vindicate; therefore, it looks beyond the suffering to the triumph that will result.[165] Others see it instead as the culmination of the abandonment Jesus experienced in this section between his disciples, the nation as a whole, and now even His heavenly Father.[166] Matthew's trajectory points toward option two, but nothing can be stated definitively.

The crowd misinterprets Jesus' words and thinks He is calling out for Elijah instead. The coming of Elijah in the future was a common understanding in Jewish thought, based on Malachi 4:5. Both John the Baptist (John 1:25) and Jesus (Matthew 16:14) were considered to be Elijah during their ministries. Jesus asserted that the Elijah prophecy was fulfilled with the coming of John the Baptist (Matthew 11:14). Again, the crowd claims that if Jesus was indeed of God, maybe Elijah would save Him. In verse fifty, Jesus "yielded up His spirit" and His earthly body finally passed.

The Ramification of the Cross (27:51-55)

At the death of Jesus, a significant shift happened with the tearing of the temple's veil. Scholars debate which veil in the temple was torn. Blomberg writes,

> The torn temple curtain probably separated the court of the Jews from the court of the Gentiles. Ephesians 2:14 seems to recall this rupture when reflecting on the abolition of the barriers between Jew and Gentile in Christ. Alternatively, if the curtain protecting the holy of holies was in view, then Matthew's point could be the new access to God provided by Jesus' atoning death (as in Heb 4:16).[167]

Regardless of which view is correct, God and Matthew attest that something has changed with Christ's death and that the temple will not play a role in the future, something that Jesus Himself had already predicted earlier in Matthew when He declared the destruction of the second temple.

The section ends with a fascinating contrast found in verse fifty-four. Matthew writes, "So when the centurion and those with him, who were guarding Jesus, saw the earthquake and the things that had happened, they feared greatly, saying, "Truly this was the Son of God!" One cannot help but notice the great contrast between this verse and verse forty-two. In verse forty-two, the religious leaders claimed that if Jesus gave them the miracle of coming down from the cross, then they would believe that He was the Son of God. In contrast, the centurion and the guards saw all of the cosmic signs that went along with the death of Jesus and understood that something significant was happening. Once again, Matthew points out Gentiles identifying with Jesus while the religious Jews denied Him, very similar to the story of the magi and King Herod in chapter two.

Theological Implications

Three significant theological implications arise in this passage. First, we see that the cross was the culmination of the plan of God. We saw in chapter one that God had established back in Genesis 3:15 this idea that the seed of the woman would crush Satan but also be wounded in the process. Passages like Isaiah 52-53 and Daniel 9:24-27 also hint at this idea of the suffering and death of the Messiah. Jesus Himself consistently told His disciples that He would die and then resurrect. The death of Jesus was always God's plan from the very beginning. God was not caught off guard in Genesis with the fall of man, and God was not caught off guard with the rejection of Jesus. It was always the plan of redemption.

However, God's plan was only possible because of Jesus' submission. Jesus was not obligated to come down from Heaven to rescue humanity, but this was an act of love from the Trinity to the lost world. At any point in Jesus' ministry, He could have returned to Heaven. He could have abandoned the mission and said, "Why should I, a perfect and sinless being, suffer for the sake of fallen humanity?" But He did not.

When Satan tempted Jesus in the wilderness to abandon His mission, He stayed strong. When they came to arrest Jesus, He remained firm. Indeed, Jesus told Peter during that time that Jesus could have called down twelve legions of angels to rescue Him (Matthew 26:53). Imagine the firepower of twelve legions of angels. The entire world would have been devastated, and Jesus would have been spared the cross. Even on the cross itself, the religious leaders practically begged Jesus to come down and abandon His mission. And yet Jesus stood firm, even to the point of physical death. Jesus came down from Heaven to save humanity, but He would not come down from the cross.

Finally, the cross was required for the salvation of the world. Jesus Himself told His disciples many times that He had to go to Jerusalem to die and would be raised from the dead. It was the entire reason that He had come down from Heaven. Paul writes in 1 Corinthians 15:3, "Christ died for our sins according to the Scriptures." In Isaiah 53, Isaiah was clear that the Suffering Servant would die for the sins of the people. Jesus Himself prayed in the Garden of Gethsemane that if there was any other way other than the cross, then to let the cup of God's wrath pass from Him (Matthew 26:39). The cross was the only way for salvation, and Jesus willingly went to the cross to pay for our sins.

Application

The cross of Jesus is the most significant idea in the entire Bible. However, the cross was not simply a theological concept. It is a personal concept. Jesus didn't only die for the world. Jesus died for you. He took on the wrath of God for you. If you have not accepted the gift of salvation that Jesus gave through His death on the cross, I implore you today to receive this miraculous gift. You can see the plan of salvation, called the Romans Road, below.

1. Romans 3:23: For all have sinned and fall short of the glory of God.
2. Romans 6:23: For the wages of sin is death.
3. Romans 5:8; But God demonstrates His own love toward us, in that while we were still sinners, Christ died for us.
4. Romans 10:9-10; That if you confess with your mouth the Lord Jesus and believe in your heart that God has raised Him from the dead, you will be saved. For with the heart one believes unto righteousness, and with the mouth confession is made unto salvation.
5. Romans 5:1: Therefore, having been justified by faith, we have peace with God through our Lord Jesus Christ.

Conclusion

We began this chapter by talking about the character of Superman. One of the things that makes Superman a superhero is his self-restraint. He could easily kill most of his opponents, yet he restrains himself from using his full power most of the time. At the cross, Jesus was similar to Superman but so much more. At any point, He could have walked off that cross. Jesus could have spoken at any point, and all His enemies would have been killed. He could have called down thousands of angels to rescue Him at any point. And yet, because Jesus showed restraint and allowed Himself to be killed and punished for our sins, we have access to salvation. We only have access to the atoning salvation of Jesus because He would not come down.

Chapter Nine

Pentecost: Permanence

I will pour out my Spirit Acts 2:17

There are very few things in life that are permanent. If you are a fan of a particular sports team, hold on and enjoy it when your team is outstanding because, eventually, it will not last. If your team is terrible, it will hopefully not last, unless you are a Cleveland Browns or New York Jets fan. If you love a favorite tv show, enjoy it because it will not last forever. We live in a world where things move very quickly, and something rarely lasts longer than a few years, let alone permanently.

I remember when I was going through my PhD defense in the Spring of 2020. I finished writing my dissertation early in the Spring and then went through the long and painful process of editing all the changes my dissertation committee wanted. Finally, it was time to defend. The only problem was that the Spring of 2020 was in the heart of the Covid pandemic. My school closed its campus during COVID-19 and moved all classes virtually. In most situations, my dissertation committee would have held my defense virtually. The only problem was that one of my committee members, Dr. Hindson, did not own a computer, so we needed to have the defense in person.

Initially, we would have the defense somewhere in the university library. Nevertheless, the night before the defense, Dr. Hindson called me and told me they were moving the defense to his house. Dr. Price and Dr. Allen also came over, and I held my defense in Dr. Hindson's basement, with everyone staying about ten feet apart. It was a very unique time. At the end of the defense, after I had passed, I remember Dr. Price, my chair, telling me, "No matter what happens from this point on, you will always be a Dr." It was a permanent thing that will never change throughout my life.

Many famous sermons have been preached throughout church history, but few have been as well-known as Peter's Sermon on the Day of Pentecost in Acts 2. The coming of the Holy Spirit, in a permanent way, was the catalyst to jumpstart that sermon. His coming changed a group of people who had hidden at Jesus' arrest into a group that could not be stopped no matter what Satan and his minions threw at them. Let's dive into the passage.

Immediate Context

When we last ended, we saw the death of Jesus on the cross at Golgotha. While we pick up the story only a few verses later in Acts 2, so much occurs during the intermission. Jesus was taken down from the cross, clearly dead, by the Roman guards. Usually, when they crucified someone, his body would have been thrown away into an unmarked grave. In contrast, they spared Jesus' body of this fate when Joseph of Arimathea, who himself was probably a member of the Sanhedrin but also was a secret follower of Jesus, went to Pilate and was given permission to bury Jesus in his brand-new tomb, which would fulfill Isaiah 53:9. He was the one that prepared Jesus' body for burial and placed His body in the tomb. Matthew notes that several women, including Mary Magdeline, were present when this occurred and thus knew where to go on Easter morning.

The following day, the high priest and the religious leaders went to Pilate and wanted Jesus' tomb put under guard to avoid anyone claiming that Jesus had risen from the dead. They understood that Jesus had claimed a future resurrection. While they did not believe Jesus' words, they were concerned that someone would steal the body and claim a resurrection. Pilate agrees to their demands and allows soldiers to secure and guard the tomb. Why does Pilate do this? He again shows that he does not want to alienate the Jewish leaders, especially during the Passover celebration.

On Easter morning, several of Jesus' female followers went to the tomb but found it empty, and they went and told the disciples. Peter and John also go to the tomb and find it empty. Jesus then began to appear to various people after His resurrection. For forty days, Jesus appeared multiple times with not only the disciples but with other followers as well. In 1 Corinthians 15, Paul outlines all the people who saw Jesus. He writes, "and that He was seen by Cephas, then by the twelve. After that, He was seen by over five hundred brethren at once, of whom the greater part remain to the present, but some have fallen asleep. After that, He was seen by James, then by all the apostles" (1 Corinthians 15:5-7).

Acts 1 then describes the ascension of Jesus back to Heaven. At this point, Jesus told the apostles to wait in Jerusalem for the promised Holy Spirit to come. Jesus did not give them a definitive timeline but told them it would occur "not many days from now" (1:5). It is through the power of this coming Spirit that will enable the disciples to serve as Jesus' witnesses to the world (1:8). After this promise and command, Jesus returned to Heaven. Through guidance and prayer, the disciples decided to replace Judas, and Mathias was chosen as his replacement. Thus, when we pick up the story in Acts 2, the disciples and followers of Jesus remained in Jerusalem in limbo until the coming of the Holy Spirit. Thankfully, they did not have to wait for long.

The Coming of the Holy Spirit (2:1-4)

God and Luke do not waste much time moving the story forward. Luke notes the timing of the chapter as occurring on the Day of Pentecost. In describing Pentecost, Schnabel writes

> Pentecost (πεντηκοστή, lit., "the fiftieth part") denotes the Festival of New Grain celebrated seven weeks or fifty days after Passover. Pentecost, the "Feast of Weeks," was the second of the three great

pilgrimage festivals of Israel. It was essentially a harvest festival, the occasion when the Jews thanked God for the gifts of the grain harvest. Since Israel had arrived at Mount Sinai in the third month after leaving Egypt (Exod 19:1), i.e., in the third month after Passover, the Festival of Pentecost was eventually connected with the celebration of the giving of the covenant and thus with the gift of the law given at Sinai.[168] Hence, if Jesus stayed on the earth after the resurrection for forty days, then the followers of Jesus only had to wait for a few short days for the coming of the Spirit. The fact that the feast is occurring also will play a role in the large crowd from various locations and languages that will be seen in a few verses.

The rest of verse one states, "They were all with one accord in one place." Two questions arise from this statement: who is the "they," and where is the "one place"? Some think the "they" only references the twelve apostles. Steven Ger writes, "While that is possible, it is difficult to reconcile with the internal evidence of the passage. Luke seems to indicate that the supernatural empowerment that morning was only granted to the twelve apostles."[169] Ger uses two principal arguments for this belief: the antecedent group was the Twelve in 1:26, and the tongues-speakers were identified in the text as Galileans. He argues this referred to the apostles, who were all Galileans, and not the large group, who probably hailed from various locations in Israel.[170]

Others believe that the group consisted of the 120 followers that were mentioned in 1:15. John Polhill writes,

> Who were the people gathered in the upper room? On whom did the Spirit descend? Was it the 120 mentioned in 1:15 or only the Twelve apostles? In 2:14, Luke discussed only the Twelve. Still, there it probably was to connect them with Peter's speech, which appealed to their special role as eyewitnesses to the resurrection (2:32). The presence of the large crowd testifying to the witness of the Spirit-filled Christians (2:6–11) would indicate that the full 120 were involved, as would the text Peter quoted from Joel that refers to women as well as men prophesying (2:17–18).[171]

Fernando similarly argues, "Some manuscripts add "the apostles" here, but these are secondary manuscripts. The great fourth-century Bible expositor, John Chrysostom, thought that the one hundred and twenty of 1:15 were there."[172] It seems best to view that the 120 were present for this event, not only the apostles.

The location of this event is also extensively debated. Ger argues that this event is happening somewhere in the Temple complex. He writes, "If this is the case the "one place" of Acts 2:1 is the upper room, it is difficult to explain why Luke provides no transitional description which maneuvers the apostles out of the house, through the city streets and into the temple complex, where they are positioned by 2:5. A more likely interpretation of the "one place" where they are assembled is the Temple courts. The term "the house" was customarily used in reference to the Temple (Acts 7:47).[173] Toussaint asserts that it is possible that they were at the Temple, but more likely, it was at a location near it.[174] This idea assumes that the crowd must have been gathered around the Temple, which is probable but unnecessary. In contrast, Polhill argues that it is most likely the upper room they were still in from chapter one. It may be near the Temple, where large crowds would assemble on a feast day.[175]

Verse two introduces the coming of the Holy Spirit and associates it with "a sound from heaven, as of a rushing mighty wind." Schnabel sees a strong connection between Jesus ascending into Heaven and the Holy Spirit coming down similarly.[176] It is apparent in the text that this is not some ordinary windstorm but is a supernatural phenomenon. The connection of the Holy Spirit with the wind is also something drawn from the Old Testament. Polhill asserts, "Wind phenomena often accompany an appearance by God in the Old Testament (cf. 1 Kgs 19:11; Isa 66:15). In Greek, *pneuma* has the double connotation of both wind and Spirit, and that connection is to be seen here. As in Ezekiel, the wind, the breath of Yahweh, is God's Spirit, which brings life in the vision of the dry bones (Ezek 37:9–14)."[177]

Verse three builds upon this with the coming of "divided tongues, as of fire, and one sat upon each of them." The association of God with fire goes throughout the Bible. In Genesis 15:17, God was represented in Abraham's vision as a burning torch. God came to Moses in Exodus 3 with the burning bush and fire. In the Exodus, God's presence and guidance for the nation was associated with a pillar of fire. When the people got to Mount Sinai, the text states, "Now Mount Sinai was completely in smoke, because the LORD descended upon it in fire" (Exodus 19:18). We already saw in 1 Kings 18 that God came down with fire to consume the altar. In the New Testament, John the Baptist declared, "I indeed baptize you with water unto repentance, but He who is coming after me is mightier than I, whose sandals I am not worthy to carry. He will baptize you with the Holy Spirit and fire" (Matthew 3:11).

The text then says that they were filled with the Holy Spirit. More on this topic will be addressed in the theological implications section. For now, it is enough to know that they are empowered by the Holy Spirit in a very special way in that they can speak other languages. It is important to note that the languages they were able to speak were legitimate ones that were spoken then, as will be seen in a few verses. It was not some heavenly language or anything like that in this instance. Some see this as a reversal of the incident of the Tower of Babel, although Luke does not directly make that connection anywhere in the passage.

Are You Drunk? (2:5-13)

Verse five shifts from the believers to the people around their location. Luke mentions that there were devout Jewish men, and presumably women, from every nation that were staying around this location. Where did these people come from? Presumably, they were Jews living outside of Jerusalem who had made the pilgrimage to celebrate the Feast of Pentecost. Schnabel notes that there could have been as many as one million pilgrims returning to Jerusalem for the celebration.[178] As a result, this was the perfect time for the foundation of the new Jesus movement to launch in Jerusalem; not only would it impact the city itself, but many of these pilgrims could then take the message back to their lands.

In verse six, this group of people gathered around the believers' location when they heard the sound. What sound did they hear? It could have been either the rushing wind itself or the sound of the believers speaking in these various languages. Regardless, a crowd quickly gathered at the location and was shocked to hear their languages being spoken to them. It was unique within Jerusalem, where Greek or Aramaic would have been the common languages spoken.

Verse seven begins to show the crowd's amazement. They cannot believe that these people can speak all of these languages. After all, most of them were from Galilee, which was not known as a region of academic success. This is well before the days of Duolingo! The statement is very similar to one later given by the Sanhedrin about Peter and John in 4:13. It would be practically impossible for these people to have learned this many languages from this many regions.

Verses eight through eleven show how many regions were represented by various languages. It was indeed a smorgasbord of nations. The nations represented were from all ends of the Roman Empire: Persia to the East, Egypt to the South, and even Rome to the West. Even someone trained as a diplomat by the Roman authorities would have had a difficult time communicating in all of these languages and dialects. Usually, a common trade language, such as Greek, would have been used to communicate with this many groups, not their own languages.

Verses twelve and thirteen show the two different reactions to this miraculous event. On the one hand, some people were amazed and wondered what this meant. They saw some supernatural phenomenon going on. On the other hand, some simply wrote off the miracle as the people being drunk. Schnabel sees this dichotomy as representative of the rest of the book. He writes, "The events triggered by the coming of the Holy Spirit upon the believers create two opposing groups, one group cautiously open to further inquiry, while the other group is openly skeptical or even hostile. This is a situation that will characterize the missionary ministry of the apostles more often than not."[179]

The First Sermon of the Early Church (4:14-35)

Peter immediately takes charge of the situation, something very different from his denial of Jesus before the crucifixion. Hearing the mocking of those who claimed the people were just drunk, Peter shows the argument makes no sense. After all, it was only nine o'clock in the morning. Outside of a raging alcoholic, very few people would have been utterly intoxicated that early in the day. Also, Peter did not mention this, but how would being drunk have answered this question? Just because someone is drunk does not mean that they all of a sudden learn to communicate in a different language that they previously did not know.

Instead, Peter argues that the miraculous event was a fulfillment of prophecy from Joel 2:28-32. The prophet Joel had predicted that God would pour His Spirit on humanity in the future. Polhill sums this prophecy up well when he writes

> For Peter the universal pouring out of the Spirit on the whole Christian group was demonstration that the end time had come. Perhaps the clearest indication that the entire 120 received the Spirit at Pentecost is Joel's inclusion of daughters as well as sons—*all* were prophesying. Joel undoubtedly had seen the Spirit's outpouring only as a gift to Israel, and perhaps many of those Jewish-Christians at Pentecost saw it the same way. The remainder of Acts clarifies that the promise applies to the Gentiles as well: it is indeed poured out on "all people.[180]

Thus, Peter saw this as a fulfillment of a promise made by God in the Old Testament, not only in Joel but also in places like Ezekiel 36:27 as well, which states, "I will put My Spirit within you and cause you to walk in My statutes, and you will keep My judgments and do them." Jesus also made many predictions about the coming of the Holy Spirit in John 14-17, such as in John 14:17 when He stated, "the Spirit of truth, whom the world cannot receive, because it neither sees Him nor knows Him; but you know Him, for He dwells with you and will be in you."

This event is a radical change from the period of the Old Testament. In the Old Testament, the Holy Spirit did not dwell inside all believers permanently. Sometimes, the Spirit would empower individuals with specific gifts, such as Samson's strength or the prophets' ability to predict the future. However, it was not a permanent indwelling and was not for all believers. With the coming of the Holy Spirit at Pentecost, Peter is declaring that the new age of the Spirit that had been promised has now arrived. The ability of believers to speak various languages was simply a sign of this coming age's arrival.

Peter then moves to verses 22-25 to discuss the coming of Jesus, who was ultimately responsible for this shift in the Spirit's methods. First, he declared that Jesus had come with miraculous powers and gifts, which should have shown that He came in the power and authority of God. Indeed, some of these people had probably been present at some of Jesus' miracles or, at the very least, had heard about them from other eyewitnesses. He then goes right to the heart of the matter, arguing that the listeners were at least partly responsible for the crucifixion, even though it was ultimately the plan of God. However, even though they were responsible for the death of Jesus, this same Jesus had been resurrected by God, showing that He had been falsely accused and was Who He had declared to be during His earthly ministry.

Peter then quoted Psalm 16:8-11, in which David spoke of a future resurrection. One might assume that David was talking about himself, yet Peter argues that David never resurrected. Instead, He argues that David was prophetically speaking about the future Messiah that would come from His line. Indeed, Peter argues that David, who he calls a prophet, recognized God's promise to him through the Davidic Covenant. Seth Postell argues that "There is little doubt the early Jewish followers of Jesus read Ps 16 as a messianic psalm. According to the Greek, David "saw in advance" (*prooraō*) the resurrection of the Messiah (Ps 15:8 LXX; Ac 2:31). Both Peter and Paul clearly regarded Ps 16 as a key psalm in their messianic apologetic since they both refer to it in their debut sermons to the Jewish people."[181] Peter's argument is then twofold. First, he argued that the resurrection of Jesus was something predicted hundreds of years in the past, using Psalm 16 as an example passage. Second, one of the significant reasons this occurred was because of God's promises to David, which is why David understood this promise.

Verses 32-33 address where Jesus went after the resurrection and why He was not present at the Day of Pentecost if He had genuinely resurrected as Peter claimed. Peter identifies that God had raised Jesus from the dead. This argument is in exact contrast to what the religious leaders thought at the cross, as we saw in the last chapter, when they believed that Jesus was a sinner being punished by God through the crucifixion. In case the people do not believe it, he argues that they all witnessed these events. Peter had seen the resurrected Jesus on multiple occasions, and the believers at Pentecost had also witnessed the risen Lord.

Peter then continues that Jesus was at the Father's right hand in Heaven. That explains His absence at Pentecost and shows His unique position. Jesus was not simply a humble rabbi or a good teacher; His authority and power were co-equal with God the Father. Because of this position and authority, He was able to send the Holy Spirit to the believers. This is a fulfillment of the promise that Jesus had given in John 14:15 and others, in which Jesus attributed that He would be involved in sending the Holy Spirit.

Peter then quotes his third Old Testament passage, Psalm 110, in which he argues that David was not talking about himself but about the future Messiah, whom Peter identified as Jesus. Jesus Himself did something very similar to this in His ministry when He quoted Psalm 110 and stated, "If David then calls Him 'Lord,' how is He his Son?" (Matthew 22:45). What both Jesus and Peter are arguing in this passage is that the Son that David was talking about was Jesus and that this Son is not simply the son of David, but also the Son of God. That is why the crowd did not respond to Jesus' assertions. Rydelnik writes, "Their failure to answer Jesus' question demonstrated that they must certainly have agreed with the messianic interpretation of Ps 110 but could not explain how the psalm could present the Messiah as deity (Lord). Although Jesus does not add any further commentary to this text, it is obvious that He too interpreted Ps 110 as about a divine Messiah."[182]

Peter then concludes the sermon with a final theological push when he states, "Therefore let all the house of Israel know assuredly that God has made this Jesus, whom you crucified, both Lord and Christ" (2:36). He sums up his entire sermon with these two ideas: Israel was responsible for Jesus' death, but ultimately God has undone that death because Jesus was God and the promised Messiah. FF Bruce sums up the push well when he writes

> The good news has been proclaimed: the witness of the apostles and the testimony of prophecy have combined to give assurance of the truth of the proclamation. The attested facts point to one conclusion: God has made the crucified Jesus both Lord and Messiah. The contrast is pointed between the treatment that Jesus received from His earthly judges and that He received from God. When He claimed to be "the Messiah, the Son of the Blessed" (Mark 14:61), His claim was rejected as false and judged to be worthy of death. But God has vindicated His claim as true, and brought Him back from death, exalting Him to the highest place that Heaven affords. His messiahship, acclaimed at His baptism, was confirmed by His resurrection; by it He was "designated Son of God in power" (Rom. 1:4). But He has been exalted not only as Messiah and Son of God, but as Lord. The first apostolic sermon concludes with the first apostolic creed: "Jesus is Lord" (cf. Rom. 10:9; 1 Cor. 12:3; Phil. 2:11)—"Lord" not only as bearer of a courtesy title but as bearer of "the name which is above every name" (Phil. 2:9).[183]

Peter leaves the audience with a choice. While they reject Jesus as Messiah again, or will they accept His position as both Messiah and Lord?

The Response at Pentecost (2:37-41)

If Peter was hoping that his sermon would impact the crowd, then verse 37 gave him an answer. Upon seeing the coming of the Holy Spirit and hearing the sermon of Peter about the Messiahship of Jesus, the audience were "cut to the heart, and said to Peter and the rest of the apostles, "Men and brethren, what shall we do?" They immediately recognized their mistake. Not only had they rejected Jesus as Messiah, but they had also allowed/promoted Him to be crucified. Schnabel writes, "Since the crowd was among those who had rejected Jesus and facilitated his crucifixion, the people find themselves in a situation that seems impossible to resolve. However, since Peter has explained that Jesus' death was part of God's plan (v. 23), there might be the possibility of avoiding God's judgment."[184]

Peter's response is not "Well, you blew it, so it's too late," but instead is "Repent, and let every one of you be baptized in the name of Jesus Christ for the remission of sins; and you shall receive the gift of the Holy Spirit" (2:38). Polhill notes that this becomes Luke's framework for the rest of the book. He writes, "Peter's response was almost programmatic in that he presented them with four essentials of the conversion experience (v. 38): repentance, baptism in the name of Jesus Christ, forgiveness of sins, and receipt of the Spirit. These four generally form a single complex throughout Luke-Acts. They are the normative ingredients of conversion."[185] It was not too late! If they repented of their sins and followed Jesus, they still had a chance to become followers. They would also be baptized in His name, showing public association with following Him, and they would also receive the Holy Spirit, just as the other believers had already received.

In verse 39, Peter describes that everyone, including their children and anyone else who the Lord calls to salvation through faith and repentance. This "altar call" establishes the framework for not only the rest of the Book of Acts but for the rest of salvation history. Acts will show that it is not just Jews who can call on the name of Jesus, but Gentiles as well will become a part of this believing community. It would take the apostles and the early church a few years to realize this, but once they did, the doors to Gentile evangelism would fly open.

Verse forty shows that Luke had only given a portion of Peter's sermon. Assumedly, the sermon was much longer and more detailed than recorded. Perhaps this is the only record that Luke had access to, or more likely, Luke wanted to give the highlights of the sermon and move on with the story. Verse forty-one concludes the passage by showing that three thousand people accepted Peter's sermon, repented of their sins, and followed in baptism in the name of Jesus. The believing community then increased from hundreds to thousands in one day. These believers also received the permanent indwelling power of the Holy Spirit, just as the initial group had received earlier that day. God had come down in the person of the Holy Spirit and now was dwelling with believers permanently, empowering them to fulfill the mission that He had called them to accomplish.

Theological Implications

The major theological implication of this section is the dramatic shift in the way the Holy Spirit works before and after Pentecost. Before Pentecost, the Holy Spirit was active in the world. He is seen at creation in Genesis 1:2. He would empower Old Testament believers for various ministries, such as constructing the Ark of the Covenant (Exodus 31:3). The kings and prophets were empowered by the Holy Spirit in unique capacities. However, it was limited to specific individuals for specific circumstances.

After Pentecost, the Holy Spirit is now "the *primary* manifestation of the presence of the Trinity among us. He is the one who is most prominently *present* with us now."[186] The Holy Spirit indwells the believer, sometimes referred to in Scripture as the baptism of the Spirit, who regenerates the believer upon salvation. The indwelling ministry of the Spirit also serves as the promise of future glorification and the mark of the true believer (Romans 8:9). He helps the believer in the process of sanctification (Romans 8:1). He empowers the believer, enlightens the believer, and enables us to live a spiritual life not in the flesh but according to the ways of God. Thus, everything changed when God came down in the Spirit at Pentecost.

Application

Acts 2 serves as a reminder of God's patient and second-chance nature. We see this with both Peter and the crowd. Peter is allowed to preach the very first sermon after the ascension of Christ. This is the same Peter who ran away from Christ in the Garden of Gethsemane after just declaring that he would die for Jesus and then backed that up by denying Jesus three times that same night, something that he had claimed he would never do when Jesus predicted it. And yet, after the crucifixion, Jesus took the time to restore Peter (John 21), and it is Peter of all people who is given the prominent speaking voice at Pentecost. God could easily have chosen another person to accomplish this task, perhaps John, the only disciple to actually come to the crucifixion. Yet, God was patient with Peter and gave him a second chance.

In ministry, we are often too quick to "throw people away" after they make a mistake. We assume that God could never use that person again after their failure. However, God is a God of second chances. This does not mean that there should not be consequences, repentance, and safeguards put into place, but it does mean that we should be careful when thinking that people are beyond God's plan. If Peter could deny Jesus three times and then preach the greatest sermon ever preached, then perhaps there is a future even though we may struggle with the impacts of the sinful condition.

We also see in this chapter that God gave the people of Jerusalem a second chance at redemption, even though many of these people were probably present just fifty days earlier and had denied and crucified Jesus. God could have easily told the apostles to leave Jerusalem. He could have said, "They had their chance, and they blew it. Move on". But He did not. Instead, God gave the very people responsible for the death of Jesus another chance at redemption. Some, like the religious leaders, chose not to take this opportunity, but many others who initially rejected it did.

This should remind us that no one is beyond redemption. It is easy for believers to think, "There is no way that man or woman will ever get saved." However, we have no idea about the conditions of someone's heart or the plans of God. Many times, the people who we would least expect to get saved are the people that God moves on the most, like the apostle Paul, who was on his way to kill Christians before his encounter with Jesus. No one is beyond the redemption of God, and we should never assume that someone cannot get saved based on the circumstances of life. God is patient, much more patient than we are in most cases, and God can work in the lives of people over time who at first rejected the Gospel but later came to accept the redemption of Jesus. Let us be faithful in sharing the Gospel with everyone and not assume who is worthy of salvation.

Conclusion

What a fantastic thing it is that the God of the universe has come down and now permanently indwells believers. We do not have to worry about losing the Holy Spirit if we have a terrible day. We do not have to worry about losing the Holy Spirit because He will indwell someone "more important" or "more influential" than us. The same Spirit present at creation, who hovered over the primeval waters (Genesis 1:2), indwells within us. The same Spirit that empowered Moses to perform the plagues, who empowered the prophets to make incredible predictions of the future, and even empowered Jesus at His baptism and was with Him throughout His entire ministry is the same Spirit that now indwells us as believers. We are foolish if we forget that God is now with us. He has come down from Heaven and now indwells us, empowers us, enables us to have spiritual gifts, and seals us with the promise of our future glorification at the return of Christ. God the Spirit has come down to be with us permanently, and He is not going anywhere!

Chapter Ten
Armageddon: Triumph

I saw Heaven opened... Revelation 19:11

Everyone loves a good ending to the story. Movies like *The Return of the King*, *Harry Potter and the Deathly Hallows*, and *The Dark Knight Rises* conclude these massive stories. I remember being in the movie theatre with my brother so many years ago, watching the finale of the *Lord of the Rings* trilogy. At this point in my life, I had never read the books, which I would eventually read a few years after the movies came out, so everything surprised me. I remember the feeling when the gates of Gondor came crashing in; it looked like all hope was lost. Then, suddenly, the horn blows, and the Rohan army shows up to save the day. The cheers in the movie theatre when all those horsemen came on screen were electric. Even in a fantasy world, seeing good win and evil defeated was still amazing.

The Book of Revelation is the ultimate conclusion to the most remarkable story ever told—a tale of 66 books that finally concludes with the final events of the Book of Revelation. The Apostle John, one of Jesus' closest disciples, was tasked with writing this concluding book. The Book of Revelation is unique in its 400 allusions to the Old Testament but not a single direct quotation. Chapter 19 serves as the book's culmination, with the final chapters of 20-22 serving as an epilogue. Let's dive in to see what John has to tell us!

Immediate Context

By the time we pick up the story in Revelation 19, a lot has happened since Acts 2. The early Church suffered great persecution but continued to flourish. They eventually branched out and began to reach the Gentiles as well as the Jews. Churches sprung up throughout the Roman Empire, mainly due to the early missionary movement under Paul, Barnabas, Timothy, and many others. Thus, the commandment of Acts 1:8 was fulfilled through this movement, and the Church was established. The Book of Acts ends with Paul being imprisoned in Rome under house arrest. He would later be released and then imprisoned again before ultimately meeting his death at the hands of a Roman executioner. Church history tells us that most of the other apostles were also martyred in various ways.

The exception to this was John. He eventually became an elder at the Church of Ephesus. Still, he was exiled to the island of Patmos (Revelation 1:9). It was here that the risen Jesus met with him and commissioned him to write the Book of Revelation. The Book of Revelation is complicated to interpret, and there are many interpretive strategies for reading the book. Some view the entire book as having occurred before 70 AD (full-preterism). Some view everything from chapters 1-18 as having already happened, but chapters 19-22 are yet to occur in the future (partial-preterism). Others view the book as forecasting the entire history of the Church and the ongoing battle between good and evil (historicist). The idealist view holds the book as a spiritual (not literal) struggle of good vs. evil. Finally, the futurist view, taken in this book, views the book as forecasting future events yet to be fulfilled and understands all of Revelation 4-22 as predictive of literal future events.

The Book moves very quickly, starting first with the commissioning of John in chapter one and then letters to the seven churches in chapters two and three. These seven churches were the original audience of the letter and were all located in Asia Minor (modern-day Turkey). John is then taken to Heaven, either physically or most likely in a vision, to see the throne room of God. At this point, God presents a seven-sealed scroll that no one has the authority to open, which causes John to weep uncontrollably. However, the Lamb of God, Jesus Christ, appears to open the scroll. Chapters 6-18 of the book consists of three cycles of judgments (seals, trumpets, bowls) and short intermissions between the judgments that either show the glory of God or give more information about some of the people and events of the Tribulation. The judgments continue to get worse and worse throughout the book, leading to the culmination of the book with the events of chapter 19. Chapter 19 begins with the marriage of the Lamb between believers and Jesus in Heaven, leading up to the events of the Second Coming beginning in verse 11.

Scripture Foundation to the Second Coming

Before we look at the passage in Revelation, it is vital to see the foundation in Scripture to the Second Coming of Jesus. The Second Coming is referred to in many of the Psalms, by the prophets, by all of the apostles, and, of course, by our Lord Himself on numerous occasions. The first person in Scripture identified as describing the Second Coming was Enoch. While the Book of Genesis does not explain these events, Jude 14-15 states, "Now Enoch, the seventh from Adam, prophesied about these men also, saying, 'Behold, the Lord comes with ten thousands of His saints, to execute judgment on all, to convict all who are ungodly among them of all their ungodly deeds which they have committed in an ungodly way, and of all the harsh things which ungodly sinners have spoken against Him.'"[187]

The Book of Daniel continues to build upon this idea of the Second Coming of Christ. In Daniel 7:13-14, Daniel writes, "I was watching in the night visions, and behold, One like the Son of Man, coming with the clouds of Heaven! He came to the Ancient of Days, and they brought Him near before Him. Then to Him was given dominion and glory and a kingdom, that all peoples, nations, and languages should serve Him. His dominion is an everlasting dominion, which shall not pass away, and His kingdom the one which shall not be destroyed." Daniel establishes that the Son of Man, Jesus' favorite term for Himself throughout the Gospels, would one day come on the clouds of Heaven, a sign of deity in the Ancient Near East, and would be given an eternal kingdom by God the Father. Jesus would establish this kingdom at His return at the Second Coming.

One of the main challenges in the Gospels is that the disciples did not recognize the idea of a First and Second Coming. Jesus told them on several occurrences that He would go to Jerusalem and be killed, but they did not accept it because they did not understand the distinction between 1st coming and 2nd coming. It is easy for us believers with a complete New Testament to look back and wonder why they could not make this distinction, but if we only had the Old Testament as they did, we probably would have had similar thoughts. Indeed, in the Dead Sea Scrolls, Jews, before the coming of Jesus, could not understand how a Messiah could both reign as King and die as a Suffering Servant. Some even thought of two Messiahs: Ben Joseph, the suffering Messiah, and Ben David, the Kingly Messiah.

It was not until after the resurrection that the apostles understood the distinctions between the First Coming and the Second Coming. Even as late as Acts 1, they believed that now that Jesus had resurrected, He would start the kingdom (Acts 1:6). Jesus responded that it was not time for the Messianic kingdom. They finally recognized this in Acts 1:9-11, which states, "Now when He had spoken these things, while they watched, He was taken up, and a cloud received Him out of their sight. And while they looked steadfastly toward Heaven as He went up, behold, two men stood by them in white apparel, who also said, "Men of Galilee, why do you stand gazing up into Heaven? This same Jesus, taken up from you into Heaven, will come like you saw Him go into Heaven." Hence, the foundation of the future Second Coming had been established.

The Arrival of the King (19:11-16)

The passage begins with the opening of Heaven. Then John sees a white horse in his vision. This vision is significant for two reasons. First, the antichrist figure in the Book of Revelation, the counterfeit, was seen riding a white horse back in 6:2 with the opening of the first seal. While he was a fake, this white horse represents the coming of the real Christ. Second, white horses also were usually considered the best. Such horses were appropriate mounts for rulers, important officials, and conquerors entering Rome in triumph.[188] That this rider is riding a white horse signifies His power and authority.

John gives the rider on the white horse many titles. First, He is called "Faithful and True" (19:11). This is in direct contrast to the Antichrist throughout the book, who is a blasphemer and deceiver, working for the great deceiver Satan. John then states, "In righteousness, He judges and makes war"

(19:11). This idea comes from two Old Testament passages. Psalm 96:13 states, "For He is coming, for He is coming to judge the earth. He shall judge the world with righteousness, and the peoples with His truth." Similarly, Isaiah 11:4 states, " But with righteousness He shall judge the poor." When Jesus comes down, He will judge the world in a righteous and just manner. Jesus knows everyone's thoughts, actions, and motivations; therefore, He can be a righteous judge.

Mounce keenly observes when he writes, "The imagery used to depict this great event reflects the Jewish tradition of a warrior Messiah more than the NT teaching of the second advent of Christ."[189] This idea of the Divine Warrior does indeed find more scriptural support in the Old Testament. However, Mounce also notes that 2 Thessalonians 1:7-8 builds upon these Old Testament passages. Paul writes, "And to give you who are troubled rest with us when the Lord Jesus is revealed from heaven with His mighty angels, in flaming fire taking vengeance on those who do not know God, and on those who do not obey the gospel of our Lord Jesus Christ." Thus, both the Old Testament and other New Testament passages build upon John's view of Jesus as the conquering Judge.

John further states, "His eyes were like a flame of fire, and on His head were many crowns" (19:12). The eyes like a flame of fire are a direct connection to Jesus' appearance in chapter one when He first commissioned John to write the book. The idea of many crowns serves as another counter to the Antichrist.[190] In chapter 6, the Antichrist figure is given a crown, but the term is different in Greek. Hindson notes, "The rider's crown is called a *Stephanos*, "victor's wreath," whereas Jesus wears the *diadema*, "royal crown. "[191] Also, both the dragon (Satan) and the beast (Antichrist) in chapters 12-13 are said to have seven and ten crowns. Hindson notes how "the fact that these diadems (crowns) are "many" totally upstages the seven crowns of the dragon and the ten crowns of the beast."[192]

John continues, "He had a name written that no one knew except Himself. He was clothed with a robe dipped in blood" (19:12-13). Some read about the robe dipped in blood and immediately think of the cross where Jesus shed His blood for the sins of the world. However, in this context, John is instead alluding to Isaiah 63:2-3. In writing about the future Divine Warrior, Isaiah said, "Why is Your apparel red, and Your garments like one who treads in the winepress? "I have trodden the winepress alone, and from the peoples no one was with Me. For I have trodden them in My anger, and trampled them in My fury; Their blood is sprinkled upon My garments, and I have stained all My robes." So, the blood on the robes does not represent Jesus' blood but the blood of His enemies that He will slay in judgment.

The winepress, which John mentioned in Revelation 14, is often used in the Bible in the context of judgment. Thomas asserts, "It is comparable to grape juice splashing on the wine treader in the winepress."[193] In the ancient world, winepresses were filled with grapes, with only a narrow spout that led to jugs being filled. The individual would then walk through the winepress, crushing the grapes. Typically, their clothes would be covered and stained with grape juice throughout this process. Isaiah and John use this analogy to show how Jesus' judgment on His enemies will similarly stain His robes. Essentially, the enemies of Jesus are like defenseless grapes ready to be crushed by divine wrath. John concludes this portion of the list of descriptions by calling Jesus the "Word of God," clearly a connection to John 1.

Perhaps the most widely interpretive verse in this passage is found in verse fourteen, which states, "And the armies in heaven, clothed in fine linen, white and clean, followed Him on white horses." The interpretive challenge is the identity of this army. Some view this as an army of angels, based upon such passages as Psalm 103:21, Psalm 148:2, Luke 2:13, and Ac 7:42.[194] Others see it as the martyrs who died during the Tribulation period. Still, others view it as the raptured Church in Heaven. It seems like they are believers instead of merely angels, as John connects the white linen given at the marriage of the Lamb earlier in the chapter with this army.

John then gives more details about Jesus, alluding to the Old Testament three more times. First, he writes, "Now out of His mouth goes a sharp sword, that with it He should strike the nations" (19:15). This is an allusion to Isaiah 11:4. However, it is also picked up by Paul in 2 Thessalonians 2:8 when he writes, "And then the lawless one will be revealed, whom the Lord will consume with the breath of His mouth and destroy with the brightness of His coming." In this context, the man of lawlessness is how Paul identified the Antichrist and how Jesus will defeat him, which is the exact context that John also addresses. The idea of the sword is once again a "one-up" on the Antichrist, who only had a bow when introduced in chapter six.

Second, John writes, "And He Himself will rule them with a rod of iron" (19:15). This is an allusion to Psalm 2:9, which states, "You shall break them with a rod of iron; You shall dash them to pieces like a potter's vessel." Mounce identifies the power behind this statement when he writes, "To rule with an iron scepter means to destroy rather than to govern in a stern fashion. The shepherd not only leads his flock to pasture but defends the sheep from marauding beasts. His rod is a weapon of retaliation. The Messiah's rod is a scepter of iron; that is, it is strong and unyielding in its mission of judgment."[195] Third, John again brings up the analogy of the winepress to show the power and judgment of Jesus.

This section concludes in verse sixteen with a final display of Jesus' power and authority. John writes, "And He has on His robe and on His thigh a name written: KING OF KINGS AND LORD OF LORDS" (19:16).

Charles Swindoll addresses these titles when he writes

> In the Old Testament, the title "king of kings" refers to the supreme earthly King. The title "Lord of lords" refers to God Himself as the supreme divine Lord. In the New Testament, Paul applies this title to God, the "only Sovereign" (1 Tim. 6:15), and John applies it to Jesus Christ (Rev. 17:14; 19:16). The case for the full deity and complete humanity of Christ—with accompanying authority over both Heaven and earth—could not be more clear. Jesus Christ is King over all who call themselves "king," and Lord above all who call themselves "lord."[196]

Thus, John concludes this section by clarifying that Jesus' coming marks a dramatic change in authority. No longer is the Antichrist and his minions in charge of the world. Instead, the true King had come down to claim His kingdom.

The Fury of the King (19:17-21)

Verses 17-18 establish the level of death and destruction that will occur with the judgment of the Second Coming. John describes an angel calling to the birds of the air, most likely vultures in the context, to ready themselves to eat the flesh of the fallen enemies of the King. Thomas shows that this statement shows the immediacy of this event, as "one of the characteristics of vultures is how incredibly swift they are in discovering and reaching a prey."[197] One cannot help but see the connection between this passage and 1 Samuel 17:44-46. There, King David similarly called the birds to be ready to eat the flesh of his enemy, Goliath. In the same way, the greater David, Jesus, will also defeat His enemy, the greater Goliath in the Antichrist and his army.

Verse nineteen describes this army of the Antichrist. John describes it as, "And I saw the beast, the kings of the earth, and their armies, gathered together to make war against Him who sat on the horse and against His army" (19:19). This is directly connected back to Revelation 16:13-16 in which Satan, the Antichrist, and the False Prophet sent out demonic spirits to rally together their armies for battle. Indeed, this passage is the only place where the title Armageddon is found in the text (16:16). The battle is set, the sides have been chosen, and the book is ready for the great battle of Armageddon between Jesus and His followers and the Antichrist and his followers.

Verses 20-21 are a conundrum; they are both the most anticlimactic verses in the Bible and maybe some of the most powerful verses. It is anticlimactic in that the "Battle of Armageddon" is not a battle, at least in how John describes it. However, they are such powerful verses because they show the magnificent power of Jesus. Jesus speaks, and the forces of the Antichrist are defeated. This event should not shock any student of the Bible. The very words of God were used to create the universe. Now, those same words are used to crush the forces of darkness.

While the members of the army of the Antichrist are slaughtered, the Antichrist and the False Prophet themselves suffer a somewhat different fate. Instead of simply being killed, they are captured and "were cast alive into the lake of fire burning with brimstone" (19:20). This is the first direct mention of the Lake of Fire in Scripture. It is mentioned four more times in Revelation 20-21. It is also distinguished from Hell since Hell is cast into the Lake of Fire (20:14). Demy describes this place when he writes, "At present, no one is in the lake of fire. The present location of all dead unbelievers since creation is called "Sheol" in the Old Testament and "hades" or "hell" in the New Testament. According to Luke 16, this place is similar to the lake of fire but not identical."[198] Perhaps the easiest way to note the distinction is that Hell is like the local jail where one is placed upon initial arrest, while the Lake of Fire is like the maximum-security penitentiary where one is placed after conviction. At the end of the chapter, Jesus has come down in triumph, defeated the forces of the Antichrist, thrown him and the False Prophet into the Lake of Fire, and established Himself as the reigning King of the world.

Theological Implications

The Book of Revelation not only shows the triumph of Jesus coming down to establish His Kingdom but also outlines the fivefold way evil is finally defeated in the book. First, the judgments of the seals, trumpets, and bowls are poured out on the earth as judgment for humanity's sinful rebellion. While these judgments are global and cosmic, Revelation 6:16-17 does show that the unbelievers that are going through the judgments at least have some knowledge that these judgments are not just global warming or some natural phenomenon but are identified by them as God's judgment, even called the wrath of the Lamb. These judgments serve as the initial thrust of judgment in the book and begin the process of the defeat of evil.

Second, the Second Coming serves as the next step in this development. Jesus defeats the forces of the Antichrist and eliminates the reign of Satan's minions over the earth. This coming down also establishes the foundation for the Millennial Kingdom in chapter twenty. Third, the binding of Satan at the beginning of chapter twenty further limits sin and deception on the earth, officially paving the way for the Millennial Kingdom. During this time, Jesus will reign and rule for 1,000 years. While sin and evil will be severely limited during this time, and Satan will not be able to tempt, there will still be the possibility of sin and death (Isaiah 65:17-25).

Fourth, the final defeat of Satan at the end of chapter twenty serves as a key checkmark in the defeat of sin and evil. After his release from his binding, Satan gathers lost humanity for one last revolt and is defeated when fire falls from Heaven, defeating him and his followers. He is cast into the Lake of Fire forever, just as his minions were in chapter nineteen. Satan, the great deceiver who was the tempter back in the Garden of Eden and has constantly, with his demonic forces, attempted to deceive and tempt humanity into rebellion against God, will finally be defeated.

However, the defeat of Satan and his demons alone is not enough to finally defeat evil forever. After all, Satan, while a tempter of evil, cannot force humanity to commit evil and did not directly cause the sinful nature of humanity. Thus, the fifth and final step in God's plan to eliminate sin and evil is found with the Great White Throne Judgment at the end of chapter twenty. At this point, all unredeemed sins throughout history will be judged, and from that point on, sin, evil, and death will be no more. Hence, the coming down of Jesus, both in judgment and victory, plays a significant role in the eventual defeat of evil throughout the Book of Revelation.

A second theological implication of this passage is the absence of annihilation in the passage. The annihilation view holds that when people die, they do not suffer eternal punishment in Hell or the Lake of Fire, but instead, their souls are annihilated by God. The view was created by those who think that eternal punishment is not something that a loving God would partake in. However, the text of Revelation clarifies that once someone is cast into the Lake of Fire, they remain there and are not annihilated. The Antichrist and the False Prophet are cast into the Lake of Fire in chapters nineteen and twenty. After 1,000 years, John says that when Satan, too, is cast into the Lake of Fire, it is already occupied. John writes, "where the beast and the false prophet are" (20:10). This seems to argue that the Lake of Fire is not some annihilation but eternal punishment, as described in many other passages.

An offshoot of this idea of punishment in this portion of the Bible is this question, "If God is good, then why does He send people to the Lake of Fire?" Many New Atheists use this question as they attack the character of God. They argue that a truly loving God would not punish people in the way that the Bible describes, and therefore, God is not good and is not worthy of worship. However, this view of God is incorrect for six reasons. First, everyone judged either throughout the Book of Revelation or in the Lake of Fire through the Great White Throne Judgment will have earned their punishment. Passages like Romans 3:10, 3:23, and 6:23 show the sinfulness of humanity. In Revelation 20:12, John writes, "And I saw the dead, great and small, standing before the throne, and books were opened. Then another book was opened, which is the book of life. And the dead were judged by what was written in the books, according to what they had done."

Consequently, God is not arbitrarily judging based on favoritism or anything like that. He specifically judges based on the actions of individuals. Also, because God is all-knowing, He knows every good and bad action of every person, so He is in the correct position to judge. God is not punishing innocents. He is not picking and choosing randomly. Everyone God punishes will have earned that punishment because of their unpaid and unrepentant sin.

Second, a good judge must hold evil accountable. If a judge just ignored crimes, he would be considered corrupt. Indeed, Deuteronomy 1:17 addressed this issue when it said, "You shall not be partial in judgment. You shall hear the small and the great alike." A good judge tries to treat everyone fairly but also must uphold the law. Indeed, large sections of the law dealt with judging correctly in Israel. Even in the Book of Revelation, the martyrs who had been murdered, "cried out with a loud voice, "O Sovereign Lord, holy and true, how long before you will judge and avenge our blood on those who dwell on the earth?" (Revelation 6:10). These believers wanted God to do what a good judge does: hold evil accountable, which God does throughout the book. Therefore, if sinners have earned judgment for their sins, God is justified in punishing them for their crimes. God would not be a good and righteous judge if He let evil go unpunished.

Third, holiness requires all sin to be treated as evil. Most people are completely fine with people like Hitler being sent to the Lake of Fire. However, they make a distinction between Hitler's sins and their sin. They will say things like, "I am a good person. I'm not as bad as _____," and always find someone else to compare their sin with, usually someone they deem more sinful. However, holiness is the standard, not a comparison with other's sins. In contrast to Holiness, all sin must be judged. Ultimately, while the consequences of sin in life might be different in eternity, all sin is created equal. All sin makes humanity unable to reach God's holiness.

Fourth, God is very patient in dealing with His judgment. For example, in Genesis 15, God gave the Canaanites 400 years to repent before sending Israel to judge them for their sin. He gave Israel and Judah a similar amount of time to repent before judgment. God was patient with Nineveh after their repentance in the book of Jonah. God could easily judge humanity after any sin was committed but shows patience to allow time for repentance and salvation. When people read the Bible and think that God is always angry and never shows patience or grace, they simply are not reading the actual story.

Fifth, God created the solution to avoid the Lake of Fire and eternal punishment. As we saw earlier, God is justified as a judge to punish sin. However, He did not stop there. God also went above and beyond His justification by personally supplying the solution to avoid judgment through the cross. Romans 8:32 states, "He who did not spare his own Son but gave him up for us all." Essentially, the Judge takes the defendant's place and takes the punishment that the defendant deserves. Jesus took the punishment that we deserved when He came down from Heaven and died on the cross.

Finally, God created a system to share the solution to avoiding the Lake of Fire. God could have made a way for salvation without sharing it with humanity. This is how the pagan gods worked in the ancient world. In Daniel 2:11, the wise men told Nebuchadnezzar, "The thing that the king asks is difficult, and no one can show it to the king except the gods, whose dwelling is not with flesh." Thus, they argued that the gods did not reveal their plans to humanity. This is not the case with the God of the Bible. God created Israel and the Church to share the message of salvation with the world. In conclusion, when people try to claim that God is not good because He judges evil, they are simply ignoring the severity of sin and the justice of holiness.

Application

When we look at passages like Revelation 19 and see our glorious future, it is beautiful. It should give us confidence in our eternal future. No matter what happens in life or what challenges we will face, if we are on the side of Jesus, we will triumph with Him at the end of time. Yes, at times, reading through prophecy can be scary. However, as my mentor, Dr. Hindson always said, "Prophecy was not written to scare us, but prepare us." While the judgment passages are difficult to read, they will ultimately occur. What this should do for us is motivate us in evangelism. One day, Jesus will return and bring judgment to the world. Our job as believers is to reach as many with the Gospel message as possible before that day comes. While we cannot save anyone, we can certainly give them every chance to accept the Gospel message so that when Jesus comes down in triumph, they can be a part of that return with us.

Conclusion

Imagine watching the events of chapter 19 unfold in a movie theatre. It would look terrible as the forces of evil with the Antichrist and the False Prophet assembling at Armageddon. One would be watching and thinking, "How could anyone defeat this powerful force"? And then suddenly, Heaven opened, and the King of Kings arrived. That major army that seemed invincible only seconds ago now is nothing in comparison to the power and majesty of Jesus. With just a statement from His mouth, the entire army is defeated, and the Antichrist and the False Prophet are thrown into the Lake of Fire. What a movie that would be! Except, it will not be a movie. No, instead, this will happen in real life. Jesus will come again. He will come down from Heaven in triumph and defeat the forces of darkness, and we, as believers, will have a front-row view of this fantastic event. The King is coming!

Conclusion

Why Does God Pick and Choose When to Come Down?

We began this book by discussing the questions people have about God coming down and intervening in their lives. While we have seen many examples of God coming down in various capacities throughout the Bible, one of the significant questions we have only briefly addressed is why God chooses to come down sometimes and not others. Why does God decide to come down and bring judgment on some people, but then it seems He lets others skate by with no judgment? Why does God choose to come down and heal some people and then let other people die?

The answer that we have in Scripture is not one that we always like to hear. The Old Testament prophet Habakkuk serves as a good illustration of this very problem. Most Christians today have probably never even read the Book of Habakkuk, unfortunately, because not only is it in the Old Testament, but it is in the Minor Prophets, one of the most overlooked portions of the Bible. Habakkuk probably served as a prophet right before the coming Babylonian Exile. In the book, Habakkuk cannot understand why God uses the pagan Babylonians to judge Judah. God answers that He is God, He can use who He wants to use, and that He will judge Babylon after He uses them to judge Judah. Hence, God can do what He chooses, ultimately, because He knows both the hearts/motivations of humanity and also knows the future.

Similarly, Isaiah 55:8 states, "For My thoughts are not your thoughts, nor are your ways My ways," says the LORD." As humans, we do not always understand the thoughts and motivations of God. Sometimes, we will see why God did certain things later in life. In my own life, I have seen this work out. For example, when I was completing my undergraduate degree at Liberty University, I tried out to be an RA twice and did not make it both times. I could not understand why God would continue to close the door in my face like that. However, after I graduated, I applied to be a Graduate Student Assistant for the School of Divinity and got the job working for my mentor, Dr. Hindson, that I would have for the next eight years. That job led me to get my master's degrees and my PhD. If I had made RA, I would not have continued with my education to that capacity, and Dr. Hindson would not have mentored me. Looking back, I am grateful that God did not open that RA door. Other times, we do not see why God does certain things, and we may never understand this side of Heaven. We must trust that God knows what He is doing, has the best motivations for us on our behalf, and that even when things do not always make sense to us, we must trust God whether He comes down in our life at this time or not.

Our Salvation is Based on God Coming Down

When it comes to why God comes down in judgment, why God heals, why God delivers, and why He does not is something that we may never know. However, we have also seen in these chapters that God's ultimate plan of redemption relies on His coming down. When humanity fell into sin in the Garden of Eden, God came down not only to bring judgment but, more importantly, to bring the provision of the hope of the future Messiah in Genesis 3:15. When the nation of Israel was in bondage and slavery and it looked like all hope was lost, God came down and delivered them out of their captivity and enabled them to form the nation of Israel in the Promised Land. Throughout the Old Testament, we saw God coming down and bringing hope and restoration to needy people.

When we turn to the New Testament, we see that God came down personally through Jesus to reconcile humanity back to Himself. Jesus Himself walked among us for decades. We saw the ultimate reversal of God coming down at the cross when Jesus could have easily come down from that cross at any moment, yet He stayed on that cross for you and me. We saw God come down again, permanently, in the coming of the Holy Spirit on the Day of Pentecost. God now lives inside of us as believers with the indwelling ministry of the Holy Spirit. Finally, we saw that God would one day come down again in the triumph of the Second Coming, bring final judgment on the forces of darkness, and usher us into the Millennial Kingdom and then the New Heavens and the New Earth for all eternity. As Isaiah the prophet stated in Isaiah 64:1, "Oh, that You would rend the heavens! That you would come down!"

Bibliography

Ackroyd, P.R. "An Interpretation of the Babylonian Exile: A Study of II Kings 20 and Isaiah 38-39." In *Studies in the Religious Traditions of the Old Testament*, 168. London: SCM, 1987.

Alexander, T. Desmond. *Exodus. Apollos Old Testament Commentary*. Downers Grove: Intervarsity Press, 2017.

Baker, David W. *Isaiah*. Edited by John H. Walton. *Zondervan Illustrated Bible Backgrounds Commentary*. Grand Rapids: Zondervan, 2009, Kindle.

Blenkinsopp, Joseph. *Isaiah 1-39. Vol. 19 of The Anchor Bible Commentary Series*. New York: Doubleday, 2000.

Blomberg, Craig. *Matthew. Vol. 22 of The New American Commentary*. Nashville: Broadman & Holman Publishers, 1992.

Bruce, F.F. *Acts. The New International Commentary On the New Testament*. Grand Rapids: Eerdmans, 1988.

Brueggemann, Walter. *1 & 2 Kings. Smyth and Helwys Bible Commentary*. Macon: Smyth and Helwys Publishing Inc, 200.

Carson, D.A. *Matthew. The Expositor's Bible Commentary*. Grand Rapids, Mich.: Zondervan, 2017, Kindle.

Constable, Thomas L. "1 Kings." In *The Bible Knowledge Commentary*, edited by J.F. Walvoord and R.B. Zuck, Wheaton: Victor Books, 1985.

Demy, Timothy J. "Lake of Fire." In *The Harvest Handbook of Bible Prophecy*, edited by Ed Hindson, Mark Hitchcock and Tim LaHaye, 212. Eugene: Harvest House Publishers, 2020.

Durham, John. *Exodus. Vol. 2 of The Word Biblical Commentary*. Grand Rapids: Zondervan, 2015.

Fanning, Buist M. *Revelation. Zondervan Exegetical Commentary on the New Testament*. Grand Rapids, Mich.: Zondervan, 2020.

Fernando, Ajith. *Acts. The NIV Application Commentary*. Grand Rapids: Zondervan, 1998.

France, R.T. *Matthew. The New International Commentary On the New Testament*. Grand Rapids: Eerdmans, 2007.

Garret, Duane A. *A Commentary on Exodus. Kregel Exegetical Library*. Grand Rapids, Mich.: Kregel Academic, 2013.

Ger, Steven. *Acts. Twenty-First Century Biblical Commentary Series.* Chattanooga, Tenn.: AMG Publishers, 2004.

Goldingay, John. *Isaiah. Understanding the Bible Commentary Series.* Grand Rapids: Baker Books, 2001, Kindle.

Goswell, Greg. "The Literary Logic and Meaning of Isaiah 38." *JSOT* 39, no. 2 (2014): 165-86.

Graves, David. *Biblical Archaeology: An Introduction with Recent Discoveries That Support the Reliability of the Bible.* 2nd ed. Vol. 1. Toronto: Electronic Christian Media, 2018.

Grudem, Wayne A. *Systematic Theology: An Introduction to Biblical Doctrine.* Grand Rapids, MI:; Zondervan Pub. House, 2004.

Hallo, W.W. and K.L. Younger, eds. "Sennacherib's Siege of Jerusalem." In *Context of Scripture: Canonical Compositions, Monumental Inscriptions and Archival Documents from the Biblical World*, 2:302-303. Leiden: Brill, 2003.

Hamilton, Victor. *Handbook on the Historical Books: Joshua, Judges, Ruth, Samuel, Kings, Chronicles, Ezra-Nehemiah, Esther.* Grand Rapids: Baker Academic, 2008.

———. *The Book of Genesis: 1-17. The New International Commentary On the Old Testament.* Grand Rapids: Eerdmans, 1990.

Hindson, Ed. *Revelation. Twenty-First Century Biblical Commentary Series.* Chattanooga, Tenn.: AMG Publishers, 2002.

House, Paul R. *1, 2 Kings. Vol. 8 of The New American Commentary.* Nashville: Broadman & Holman Publishers, 1995.

Johnson, Alan F. *Revelation. The Expositor's Bible Commentary.* Grand Rapids, Mich.: Zondervan, 2006, Kindle.

Kaiser Jr. Walter. *Exodus. The Expositor's Bible Commentary.* Grand Rapids, Mich.: Zondervan, 2017, Kindle edition.

Keener, Craig S. *Revelation. The NIV Application Commentary.* Grand Rapids: Zondervan, 1999.

Konkel, August H. *1 & 2 Kings. The NIV Application Commentary.* Grand Rapids: Zondervan, 2006.

Lamb, David. *1-2 Kings. The Story of God Bible Commentary.* Grand Rapids, Mich.: Zondervan, 2021.

Maier III, Walter. *1 Kings 12-22. Concordia Commentary.* St. Louis: Concordia Publishing House, 2019.

Mangum, Douglas, Miles Custis and Wendy Widder. *Genesis 1-11*. Bellingham: Lexham Press, 2012.

Mathews, K.A. *Genesis 1-11:26*. Vol. 1A of *The New American Commentary*. Nashville: Broadman & Holman Publishers, 1996.

McConville, J. Gordon. *Isaiah. Baker Commentary on the Old Testament: Prophetic Books*. Grand Rapids: Baker Academic, 2023.

Morris Leon. *The Gospel According to Matthew. The Pillar New Testament Commentary*. Grand Rapids: Eerdmans, 1992.

Motyer, J A. *The Prophecy of Isaiah: An Introduction and Commentary*. Downers Grove, Ill.: InterVarsity Press, 1993.

Mounce, Robert H. *Revelation. The New International Commentary On the New Testament*. Grand Rapids: Eerdmans, 1997.

Osbourne, Grant. *Matthew. Zondervan Exegetical Commentary on the New Testament*. Grand Rapids, Mich.: Zondervan, 2010.

Oswalt, John. *The Book of Isaiah: 1-39. The New International Commentary On the Old Testament*. Grand Rapids: Eerdmans, 1986.

Patterson, Richard. *1-2 Kings. The Expositor's Bible Commentary*. Grand Rapids, Mich.: Zondervan, 2009.

Pettus, David. "Reading a Protoevangelium in the Context of Genesis." *Eruditio Ardescens* 1, no. 2 (2014): 2-3.

Polhill, John B. *Acts*. Vol. 26 of *The New American Commentary*. Nashville: Broadman & Holman Publishers, 1992.

Postell, Seth D. "Genesis 3:15: The Promised Seed." In *The Moody Handbook of Messianic Prophecy: Studies and Expositions of the Messiah in the Old Testament*, edited by Michael Rydelnik and Edwin Blum, 241. Chicago: Moody Publishers, 2019.

———. "Psalm 16: The Resurrected Messiah." In *The Moody Handbook of Messianic Prophecy: Studies and Expositions of the Messiah in the Old Testament*, edited by Michael Rydelnik and Edwin Blum, 513. Chicago: Moody Publishers, 2019.

Reeves, Rodney. *Matthew. The Story of God Bible Commentary*. Grand Rapids, Mich.: Zondervan, 2017.

Roberts, J.J.M. "Prophets and Kings: A New Look at the Royal Persecution of Prophets against Its Near Eastern Background." In *God so Near: Essays On Old Testament Theology in Honor of Patrick d. Miller*, edited by Brent A. Strawn and Nancy R. Bowen, 341-54. University Park: Pennsylvania State University Press, 2002.

Ross, Allen P. "Genesis." In *The Bible Knowledge Commentary*, edited by J.F. Walvoord and R.B. Zuck, Wheaton: Victor Books, 1985.

Ross, Jillian. "Exodus." In *The Evangelical Study Bible*, Nashville: Thomas Nelson, 2023.

Endnotes

[1] This book will not address Adam's historicity but assumes that he was a historical figure and that the events of Genesis 3 occurred in history.

[2] This assumes that the years in Genesis 1-11 are the same as those of humans today. Some scholars argue that the years in Genesis 1-11 were inflated as legendary or mythological because of their duration. Others argue that man lived longer prior to the flood and that ages began to decrease rapidly after that point.

[3] John H. Walton, *Genesis*, The NIV Application Commentary (Grand Rapids, MI: Zondervan, 2001), 204-209. Walton does not deny that Scripture later teaches that this figure is Satan but does argue that there is no way that the original audience of Genesis would have been able to know this.

[4] Douglas Mangum, Miles Custis, and Wendy Widder, *Genesis 1–11*, Lexham Research Commentaries (Bellingham, WA: Lexham Press, 2012), Ge 3:1–24. One of the challenges in Old Testament studies is knowing what an original audience would have believed at various times throughout Israelite history. Because of the length of time between them and us, there are very few documents, either found or still in existence, outside of the Old Testament itself that gives us any hint of what they believed prior to about 400 BC. Perhaps one day archaeology will provide more answers to this but currently all we have in many of these texts is what is found in the Old Testament.

[5] K. A. Mathews, *Genesis 1-11:26*, vol. 1A, The New American Commentary (Nashville: Broadman & Holman Publishers, 1996), 234. There is nothing in the text of Genesis that mentions any other creatures with the ability to talk in this manner. Therefore, it would be likely that Eve would have understood that this creature was very different than the rest of creation.

⁶ Mathews, 232. The creation of Satan is not directly mentioned in the Bible. Why God did not portray this story is Scripture is unknown.

⁷ It is unclear in the text if Eve had heard the command directly from God. In Genesis 2, the command was given to Adam prior to the creation of Eve and is never repeated in the text once she is created. It is unknown if God communicated the restriction with her or if Adam was the one who told her and possibly added the restriction.

⁸ Walton, 205. Satan is very crafty in that he is a master of manipulation. He uses just enough truth to make something seem legitimate. It is only after everything falls apart that we realize the truth that he tells is missing key elements.

⁹ Mangum, Ge 3:1–24.

¹⁰ Walton, 206. Indeed, it would be impossible for God to blame Adam if he had truly been deceived by Eve. If Adam had not been present in some capacity and had just received the fruit from Eve without knowledge of its origin, then it would not have his fault. That God holds him accountable for the sin seems to show that he had knowledge of the fruit's origin and chose to disobey God's commands willingly.

¹¹ Mathews, 238.

¹² Gordon Wenham, *Genesis 1-15*, vol. 1, The Word Biblical Commentary (Grand Rapids: Zondervan, 2014), 76. Sin usually works in this way. It promises greatness, but once it has been done, rarely delivers on that greatness but instead leads to negative consequences.

¹³ Walton, 224. Many just assume that because God was doing this at this moment that it was something that He regularly did, but that is a bit of an assumption.

¹⁴ Mathews, 244. The assumption that the snake used to walk and not slither is just that, an assumption that might be possible but is not definitive in the text.

¹⁵ Victor Hamilton, *The Book of Genesis: 1-17*, The New International Commentary On the Old Testament (Grand Rapids: Eerdmans, 1990), 204. This is hard to argue with the continued warnings of death throughout these early chapters. Adam, although he might not have completely understood what death was like people after the fall would, had been warned about it by God.

¹⁶ Walton, 229. It is interesting that there is a sacrifice with Cain and Abel in the next chapter, although the regulations for this sacrifice was not given in the text.

[17] Hamilton, 207.

[18] Walton, 229. While this is certainly true and is a part of the provision, it does not automatically mean that it cannot be viewed as a sacrifice.

[19] Mathews, 255. One must remember that Moses' original audience was not living during the time of Adam but much later and therefore could have recognized some of these connections that even Adam and Eve would possibly not have made.

[20] David Pettus, "Reading a Protoevangelium in the Context of Genesis," ERUDITIO ARDESCENS 1, no. 2 (2014): 2.

[21] Walton, 226.

[22] Pettus, 2.

[23] John H. Sailhamer, *Genesis*, The Expositor's Bible Commentary (Grand Rapids: Zondervan, 2008), 91. This is important. One cannot simply read Genesis 3:15 in a vacuum. Moses builds on this idea of seed throughout the rest of Genesis.

[24] Seth D. Postell, "Genesis 3:15: The Promised Seed," in *The Moody Handbook of Messianic Prophecy: Studies and Expositions of the Messiah in the Old Testament* (Chicago, IL: Moody Publishers, 2019), 241.

[25] Pettus, 3. Paul did not cite this passage in a traditional sense, but the language here is pretty clearly tied back to Genesis 3:15

[26] Mathews, 466.

[27] Wenham, 238.

[28] Hamilton, 350. While taking away a lingua franca would have certainly impacted society, it seems unlikely that it would have done the type of damage described in the text. The people have to divide into different ethnic groups based upon this language divide. Thus, it seems that new languages would have been created through this process, not simply a temporary loss of communication.

[29] Mathews, 477–478. While the number of years this incident occurs after the great flood is not directly addressed, if it occurred relatively quickly after this event, then the population would not have been such a large number that would make this act impossible.

[30] Walton, 372. In a modern world, we do not even think about not having access to construction supplies. However, in the ancient world, a lack of trains, planes, etc. would have limited access to these types of construction supplies if they were not present around the construction site.

31 Wenham, 239.

32 Walton, 374. Some of these buildings still exist in the Middle East today. My brother, while serving in Iraq, saw the remains of one of these structures.

33 Allen P. Ross, "Genesis," in *The Bible Knowledge Commentary: An Exposition of the Scriptures*, ed. J. F. Walvoord and R. B. Zuck, vol. 1 (Wheaton, IL: Victor Books, 1985), 44.

34 Walton, 376-377.

35 Walton, 377. This was a common idea throughout the ancient world for centuries. The pagan gods were treated as basically divine humans, with the same needs, wants, and desires as mankind, including the need for food and sexual unions with either other gods or even humanity.

36 Hamilton, 353. This early in history, a massive, fortified city would have been a huge military advantage. Siege equipment and the other necessary equipment needed to defeat a fortified city would have been difficult to gather and would have made the town almost impregnable to foreign invasion.

37 God did not forget the covenant He had made. The text argues that God is about to intervene on behalf of His people because of that covenant.

38 Douglas K. Stuart, *Exodus*, vol. 2, The New American Commentary (Nashville: Broadman & Holman Publishers, 2006), 108.

39 John Durham, *Exodus*, vol. 3, The Word Biblical Commentary (Grand Rapids: Zondervan, 2015), 30. Throughout the Bible, God rarely meets with people at the moment that they expect. Instead, He reaches out based upon His own timetable, not based upon when we are ready.

40 Horeb and Mount Sinai are viewed almost interchangeably throughout the Bible. Alexander argues that "the way in which the names Sinai and Horeb are used suggests that Sinai is a precise location and Horeb a more general one." T. Desmond Alexander, *Exodus*, Apollos Old Testament Commentary (Downers Grove: Intervarsity Press, 2017), 85.

41 Walter Kaiser, Jr., *Exodus*, The Expositor's Bible Commentary (Grand Rapids: Zondervan, 2017), loc. 2251-2253. Indeed, Moses probably wrote the majority of this book while the nation was present at this very location. The Israelites stayed at Mount Sinai for a significant amount of time in the story.

42 Stuart, 109. In such a dry and humid climate, the bush would have normally burnt up in a matter of minutes, possibly an hour at the longest.

⁴³ Stuart, 112.

⁴⁴ Stuart, 113–114.

⁴⁵ Kaiser, loc. 2307. Moses would see this again later in Exodus when he wanted to see God's face and was told that it would kill him.

⁴⁶ Christopher Wright, *Exodus*, The Story of God Bible Commentary (Grand Rapids: Zondervan, 2021), 92. It is easy to forget when reading from Genesis into Exodus to forget the sheer amount of time that happens between the books. Over 400 years is a very long time for God to have been silent, from the time of Joseph to the burning bush. It would have been easy for the people to have assumed God had forgotten or abandoned them.

⁴⁷ Alexander, 85. They were about as far away from the Promised Land as one could possibly be in their circumstance. Instead of the blessing of the Promised Land, they had only felt the pain of bondage for centuries.

⁴⁸ Duane A. Garret, *A Commentary on Exodus*, Kregel Exegetical Library (Grand Rapids: Kregel Academic, 2013), 203. Moses himself had seen this problem forty years earlier and had tried to stop it in his own power. Now, he would see it from God's perspective.

⁴⁹ Wright, 95.

⁵⁰ Alexander, 85. God was taking ownership over the nation. Just as they were "His" people, He would deliver them as "their" God.

⁵¹ Stuart, 118. Egypt was one of the strongest nations in the world during this time and Pharaoh would have been considered one of if not the most powerful people in the world.

⁵² Kaiser, loc. 2330-2332. While Moses would be the one to confront Pharaoh, he did not have to do that in his own power and authority. He was simply serving as the ambassador of YHWH. This would have given him a little confidence as he was not rallying some type of slave revolt, but instead of merely declaring the words of YHWH and performing the miracles that YHWH empowered him to do.

⁵³ Stuart, 118.

⁵⁴ Stuart, 118.

⁵⁵ Garret, 205.

⁵⁶ Kaiser, loc. 2388. Moses was not wrong from a human perspective. He was eighty years old. However, he failed to understand that God had been preparing him for this mission for those eighty years and that Moses would live for another forty years.

⁵⁷ God answered this possible objection later in Exodus 4:19 when He told Moses that the men who were seeking his life had all died.

⁵⁸ Alexander, 87. While God had used this to train Moses in the Egyptian ways that would allow him to accomplish many of his tasks, it did limit his interaction with the people. He was signing up to lead a people that he really did not know in any meaningful way.

⁵⁹ Kaiser, loc. 2390. For most of us, this would have been the very first objection. Moses never even brought it up.

⁶⁰ Stuart, 118.

⁶¹ Alexander, 87. One could ultimately argue that the miracle of the burning bush itself was the sign as it was the miracle that had drawn Moses into the conversation.

⁶² Kaiser, loc. 2426. The Exodus is both a physical rescue, but more importantly it is also a spiritual rescue for the nation. They had to first be rescued before God could then establish the nation in the Promised Land and give them the Mosaic Law.

⁶³ Stuart, 119.

⁶⁴ Garrett, 206.

⁶⁵ Kaiser, loc. 2551.

⁶⁶ Jilian Ross, "Exodus," in *The Evangelical Study Bible* (Nashville: Thomas Nelson, 2023),107-108.

⁶⁷ Kaiser, loc. 2526. Ultimately, Pharaoh was unwilling to allow the Israelite to do anything, probably because their numbers were so great that any movement would have made it much more difficult for the Egyptians to remain in control.

⁶⁸ Stuart, 125.

⁶⁹ Stuart, 126. Moses probably had no idea the type of devastation that he would be bringing on the nation of Egypt. Had God told him all that would occur, Moses would have been most likely terrified that Pharaoh would try to kill him.

⁷⁰ Alexander, 94.

⁷¹ Wright, 113. How much wealth and resources the Israelites had in slavery is unknown, it is unlikely that they had much in terms of wealth prior to the Egyptians handing over their wealth.

72 August H. Konkel, *1 and 2 Kings*, The NIV Application Commentary (Grand Rapids, MI: Zondervan, 2006), loc. 3293. Droughts in the ancient world were catastrophic. Water could not be flown in like today so a long drought would decimate the society. Many people would move, like Jacob and his family in Genesis, and those that remained could have to battle for what water could be found.

73 This Obadiah is not to be confused with the prophet Obadiah. Scholars agree that these two men shared the same name.

74 David Lamb, *1-2 Kings*, The Story of God Bible Commentary (Grand Rapids: Zondervan, 2021), 229. In a time of turmoil with the drought, only the wealthy or the well-connected would have been able to save these prophets and provide for them.

75 Thomas L. Constable, "1 Kings," in *The Bible Knowledge Commentary: An Exposition of the Scriptures*, ed. J. F. Walvoord and R. B. Zuck, vol. 1 (Wheaton, IL: Victor Books, 1985), 525. By this point, the Northern Kingdom had been living in apostasy for decades. Elijah had an uphill battle to climb to try to get the country to turn back to YHWH, especially with the king and queen promoting Baal worship.

76 Paul R. House, *1, 2 Kings*, vol. 8, The New American Commentary (Nashville: Broadman & Holman Publishers, 1995), 216.

77 Konkel, 3293. Working for a pagan would already be tough, but working for a pagan king that could have you killed for worshipping YHWH would be an entirely difficult phenomenon for Obadiah.

78 Richard Patterson, *1-2 Kings*, The Expositor's Bible Commentary (Grand Rapids: Zondervan, 2009), 287.

79 Patterson, 287.

80 Donald Wiseman, *1, 2 Kings*, vol. 9, Tyndale Old Testament Commentaries (Downers Grove: IVP Academic, 2008), 168. With both men accusing each other of causing the drought, a tiebreaker is needed. The challenge of Carmel will serve as the definitive mark of which deity is actually in charge, YHWH or Baal.

81 Konkel, 3294.

82 Wiseman, 168. Indeed, the Mosaic Law had established that YHWH would bless the nation with fruitful crops if they stayed faithful to Him. That they are in a drought should not be a surprise to anyone who had paid attention to the Law.

83 Walter Maier III, *1 Kings 12-22*, Concordia Commentary (St. Louis: Concordia Publishing House, 2019), 1393.

⁸⁴ Konkel, 3294. Jezebel surely would have thought that her prophets would have been able to overcome Elijah. After all, there were hundreds of them and Elijah was just one man. What she did not recognize was that it was not the number of prophets, but which God was worshipped that ultimately mattered.

⁸⁵ Constable, 526.

⁸⁶ More on this will be addressed in the theological implications.

⁸⁷ Hamilton, *Handbook*, 432.

⁸⁸ Patterson, 350. Elijah is trying to get the people to realize that the god that the prophets had created was no different than a human, whereas YHWH was completely unique.

⁸⁹ Konkel, 3295-3296.

⁹⁰ Walter Brueggemann, *1 & 2 Kings*, Smyth and Helwys Bible Commentary (Macon: Smyth and Helwys Publishing Inc., 2000), 226.

⁹¹ Chapter thirty-eight must occur first chronologically as God declares to Hezekiah that the Assyrian invasion that occurs in chapters thirty-six and thirty-seven will happen in the future (v. 6). Chapter thirty-nine mentions Hezekiah's recovery from sickness, so that must occur after events of chapter thirty-eight. Chapter thirty-nine must occur before the events of chapters thirty-six and thirty-seven because Merodach-Baladan, the Babylonian ruler mentioned, was out of power by the time of the Assyrian invasion of Israel.

⁹²Scholars calculate this date by backtracking the fifteen years given to Hezekiah from when scholars generally date his death.

⁹³ Edward Young, *The Book of Isaiah, Chapters 19-39*, vol. 2 (Grand Rapids, MI: Eerdmans, 1969), 509. Goswell also points out that the belief that Hezekiah's tears were not for his death but the death of the Davidic line was found in both Josephus and the Talmud. Greg Goswell, "The Literary Logic and Meaning of Isaiah 38," *JSOT* 39, no. 2 (2014): 167.

⁹⁴ At first glance, this could be seen as either a lie or a false prophecy from Isaiah since Hezekiah did not die then. However, it becomes clear throughout the Old Testament that when Yahweh makes a judgment claim, He could reverse it many times if the judged party turned away from their sin. The most remarkable example of this in the Old Testament is the book of Jonah, where Yahweh does not indicate any chance for repentance and yet stays His judgment when the Assyrians turn from their wickedness.

⁹⁵ David W. Baker, *Isaiah*, ed. John H. Walton, *Zondervan Illustrated Bible Backgrounds Commentary* (Grand Rapids: Zondervan, 2009), loc. 4761.. Other

prophets were not so fortunate in giving negative news to kings of Israel and Judah, such as Jeremiah and Elijah, who were both persecuted for their words. Hezekiah's father, Ahaz, had ignored Isaiah's warnings in chapter seven. Tradition also says that Isaiah may have later died at the orders of Manasseh.

[96] J. Gordon McConville, *Isaiah*, Baker Commentary on the Old Testament: Prophetic Books (Grand Rapids, MI: Baker Academic, 2023), 430. It may be that Hezekiah was turning away from God. It may also be that he was so weak from his ailment that he had no strength to do anything else.

[97] John Goldingay, *Isaiah*, Understanding the Bible Commentary Series (Grand Rapids, MI: Baker Books, 2001), loc. 4300.

[98] John D.W. Watts, *Isaiah 34-66*, Vol. 25 of The Word Biblical Commentary (Waco: Word Books, 1987), 584.

[99] Paul D. Wegner, *Isaiah*, (Downers Grove: InterVarisity Press, 2021), 366. Theologically, Hezekiah knows that YHWH has not forgotten about him. However, when under pressure, people tend to think more practically and all Hezekiah can think about is why YHWH would allow him to die.

[100] J A. Motyer, *The Prophecy of Isaiah: An Introduction and Commentary* (Downers Grove: InterVarsity Press, 1993), 263.

[101] John N. Oswalt, *The Book of Isaiah: 1-39*, The New International Commentary On the Old Testament (Grand Rapids: Eerdmans, 1998), 676.

[102] Young, The Book of Isaiah, 512. This is similar to the problem that Hezekiah's father Ahaz had dealt with in chapter seven. The Messianic line was constantly under attack throughout history.

[103] Gary V. Smith, Isaiah 1–39, ed. E. Ray Clendenen, The New American Commentary (Nashville: B & H Publishing Group, 2007), 640.

[104] Critical scholars completely downplay the predictive nature of these events and argue that the predictions were legendary stories that we compiled after the events to give glory to Israel's God.

[105] Critical scholars view these signs as legendary, often associated with miraculous events. For example, Roberts states, "In semi-legendary narratives about famous prophets, these signs sometimes have miraculous qualities...Prophets may occasionally have claimed the power to give such signs." J.J.M. Roberts, "Prophets and Kings: A New Look at the Royal Persecution of Prophets against Its Near Eastern Background," in *God so Near: Essays On Old Testament Theology in Honor of Patrick D. Miller*, ed. Brent A. Strawn and Nancy R. Bowen (University Park: Pennsylvania State University Press, 2002), 344.

[106] The text of the Taylor Prism, the Assyrian account of the invasion, states, "As for Hezekiah, the Judean, I besieged forty-six of his fortified walled cities and surrounding smaller towns, which were without number. Using packed-down ramps and applying battering rams, infantry attacks by mines, breeches, and siege machines, I conquered (them). I took out 200,150 people, young and old, male and female, horses, mules, donkeys, camels, cattle, and sheep, without number, and counted them as spoil. He himself, I locked up within Jerusalem, his royal city, like a bird in a cage. I surrounded him with earthworks, and made it unthinkable for him to exit by the city gate." W.W. Hallo and K.L. Younger, eds., "Sennacherib's Siege of Jerusalem," in *Context of Scripture: Canonical Compositions, Monumental Inscriptions and Archival Documents from the Biblical World* (Leiden: Brill, 2003), 2:302-3.

[107] That Sennacherib sieged Lachish is supported by Assyrian reliefs of the event. David Graves, *Biblical Archaeology: An Introduction with Recent Discoveries That Support the Reliability of the Bible*, 2nd ed. (Toronto: Electronic Christian Media, 2018), 1:171.

[108] Barry G. Webb, *The Message of Isaiah*, The Bible Speaks Today (Downers Grove: IVP Academic, 1997), 148-149. While Satan is not mentioned in the text, one can only assume that he was present for this huge moment in Israel's history.

[109] Motyer, *Isaiah*, 250. Isaiah had also made a similar warning in chapters 28-32, trying to get Hezekiah to trust YHWH over trusting national alliances.

[110] Interestingly, one hundred years later, the Babylonians could have made this very argument against the nation. They would have been entirely accurate in their theological intimidation as God had turned and empowered Babylon to take the country into exile.

[111] Smith, *Isaiah 1-39*, 602.

[112] Joseph Blenkinsopp, *Isaiah 1-39, Volume 19 in* The Anchor Bible Commentary Series (New York: Doubleday, 2000), 470. Hezekiah was a Godly king that was well-liked in the nation, thus preventing the people from trying to assassinate him. Had the situation happened with a different Judean king, it is possible that the people would have tried something like this to avoid Assyria's wrath.

[113] Motyer, *Isaiah*, 251. While Rabshakeh may have just assumed that Judah's deity would claim to save them, and that is why he makes the claim, it seems very specific, almost as if he has been told about the prophecy that God made to Hezekiah in chapter 38 before the invasion. It is possible that captured Jewish leaders from some of the other cities may have told the Assyrians about

the prophecy, which would explain why the Rabshakeh was so adamant in his verbal assaults on the promise of deliverance by Judah's God.

[114] P. R. Ackroyd, "An Interpretation of the Babylonian Exile: A Study of II Kings 20 and Isaiah 38–39," in *Studies in the Religious Tradition of the Old Testament* (London: SCM, 1987), 168.

[115] Smith, *Isaiah 1-39*, 605. Indeed, the Rabshakeh was a master negotiator. He knew precisely when to threaten with the stick and when to offer the carrot. Judah's faith was a testament to Hezekiah's leadership and trust in God.

[116] Oswalt, *The Book of Isaiah, Chapters 1–39*, 641.

[117] Young, *The Book of Isaiah, Chapters 19–39*, 470. Assyrian had no reason to think that YHWH was any different than the other pagan gods. After all, the Northern Kingdom had already been destroyed and they had conquered much of Judah. In their mind, if YHWH was really that powerful, then He would have never have let His nations be attacked and defeated. What they did not realize is that YHWH was using Assyria to punish the countries, but only to a point.

[118] Oswalt, *The Book of Isaiah, Chapters 1–39*, 645.

[119] Smith, *Isaiah 1-39*, 611. While the victory would occur, the nation had still suffered extreme devastation with the invasion and therefore in many ways was very similar to the people when they would return to the land hundreds of years later after the Babylonian Exile.

[120] Blenkinsopp, *Isaiah 1-39*, 476.

[121] Hans Wildberger, *Isaiah 28-39*, Continental Commentary Series (Minneapolis: Augsburg Books, 2002), 421.

[122] Watts, *Isaiah 34-66*, 36.

[123] Young, *Isaiah 19-39*, 484. Hezekiah never questions whether YHWH can bring the victory, only if He would choose to do it.

[124] A bit of hyperbole is present in the text, as not all the nations of the earth would hear about Judah's deliverance. However, because of Assyria's immense power and prestige, many countries in the ANE could have heard about their defeat at the hand of Judah's God. One could argue that the nations did not turn to God, and therefore, Hezekiah's argument failed, but the nation's failure to turn to God could be seen more as a result of their spiritual blindness than a failure on any part of God.

[125] Goldingay, *Isaiah*, 4201. Throughout the Bible, it is never a good end for the human who puts himself in the place of God. Pharaoh believed he

was greater than God and had his kingdom decimated. King Herod Agrippa in the New Testament was called a deity in a prideful manner and killed. Putting oneself in the place of God usually leads to a quick death.

126 Baker, *Isaiah*, loc. 4712.

127 Young, *The Book of Isaiah: 19-39*, 480.

128 Rodney Reeves, *Matthew*, The Story of God Bible Commentary (Grand Rapids: Zondervan, 2017), 54.

129 It is possible that Luke's account was not known as much in the early church and that he only heard these stories through his research (Luke 1:1-4), perhaps even a direct eyewitness account from Mary herself.

130 Grant Osbourne, *Matthew*, Zondervan Exegetical Commentary on the New Testament (Grand Rapids: Zondervan, 2010), 54. This is why this Matthew has a problem. He cannot simply dump her. He would have to go through a legal process that he knows would eventually get out unless extreme care was taken by both sides.

131 D.A. Caron, *Matthew*, The Expositor's Bible Commentary (Grand Rapids: Zondervan, 2017), loc. 4411. We do not know how Mary's parents took this news. Scripture does not record any angelic visitor to them. Perhaps they trusted their daughter and believed her story or perhaps they simply tried to make the best of a difficult situation.

132 Michael J. Wilkins, *Matthew*, The NIV Application Commentary (Grand Rapids, MI: Zondervan Publishing House, 2004), 74.

133 Craig Blomberg, *Matthew*, vol. 22, The New American Commentary (Nashville: Broadman & Holman Publishers, 1992), 58.

134 R.T. France, *Matthew*, The New International Commentary On the New Testament (Grand Rapids: Eerdmans, 2007), 101.

135 This is not arguing that the Holy Spirit created Jesus but that the Holy Spirit was involved in making the human body that Jesus would reside in for His time on earth. Jesus, as a member of the Trinity, has always existed.

136 France, 101.

137 Osbourne, 104. This is an example of God using a common belief in the ancient world to communicate His message.

138 Wilkins, 77. The stigma of an adultery, especially in Israel, would have been life changing, to the point that Mary and Joseph would have dealt with the gossip for the rest of their lives.

139 Blomberg, 59.

140 Carson, loc. 4461.

141 Michael A. Rydelnik, "Isaiah 7:1–16: The Virgin Birth in Prophecy," in *The Moody Handbook of Messianic Prophecy: Studies and Expositions of the Messiah in the Old Testament*, ed. Michael Rydelnik and Edwin Blum (Chicago, IL: Moody Publishers, 2019), 816.

142 Wilkins, 81.

143 Osbourne, 107.

144 Carson, loc. 4608. This is direct opposition to the idea of Mary's perpetual virginity that is held by some. The New Testament is clear that Mary had other children after Jesus.

145 Wayne A. Grudem, *Systematic Theology: An Introduction to Biblical Doctrine* (Grand Rapids, MI: Zondervan Pub. House, 2004), 529.

146 Grudem, 530.

147 Grudem, 530.

148 Blomberg, 414. The point of this weapon was to inflict as much torture as humanly possible without killing the person.

149 Wilkins, 895.

150 Leon Morris, *The Gospel According to Matthew*, The Pillar New Testament Commentary (Grand Rapids: Eerdmans, 1992), 711.

151 France, 713. The Romans and the Jews had a very tense relationship that seemed to always be on the brink of rebellion.

152 Osborne, 1492.

153 France, 716.

154 France, 716. Peter would eventually be restored by Jesus after the resurrection and would become one of the leaders of the early church. However, at this point, he was in hiding. John was the only apostle that showed up for the crucifixion.

155 Morris, 714.

156 Osborne, 1493.

157 Blomberg, 416. Crucifixion was feared throughout the ancient world. It was a horrible way to die. In fact, it was so horrid that Roman citizens were not allowed to be crucified, which is why Paul did not suffer this fate even though Peter, a non-Roman citizen, did.

[158] Morris, 713. Many see Matthew using the Old Testament to such an extent because he was writing to a Jewish audience that would have been much more versed in the Old Testament than a gentile audience. In Acts, Paul similarly uses the Old Testament more when speaking to Jewish audiences than when speaking to Gentiles.

[159] Wilkins, 899.

[160] Osborne, 1496.

[161] Morris, 716.

[162] David L. Turner, *Matthew*, Baker Exegetical Commentary on the New Testament (Grand Rapids: Baker Academic, 2008), 664.

[163] Reeves, 546.

[164] Morris, 720. Some think that it might have been some type of lunar eclipse. Even so, the timing of the eclipse lining up precisely with Jesus' crucifixion was no random coincidence if that is truly how the darkness occurred.

[165] Osborne, 1501.

[166] Osborne, 1501.

[167] Blomberg, 421.

[168] Eckhard J. Schnabel, *Acts*, Zondervan Exegetical Commentary on the New Testament (Grand Rapids: Zondervan, 2012), 188.

[169] Steven Ger, *Acts*, Twenty-First Century Biblical Commentary Series (Chattanooga: AMG Publishers, 2004), 37.

[170] Ger, 37.

[171] John B. Polhill, *Acts*, vol. 26, The New American Commentary (Nashville: Broadman & Holman Publishers, 1992), 97.

[172] Ajith Fernando, *Acts*, The NIV Application Commentary (Grand Rapids, MI: Zondervan Publishing House, 1998), 87.

[173] Ger, 37.

[174] Stanley D. Toussaint, "Acts," in *The Bible Knowledge Commentary: An Exposition of the Scriptures*, ed. J. F. Walvoord and R. B. Zuck, vol. 2 (Wheaton, IL: Victor Books, 1985), 357.

[175] Polhill, 96–97.

[176] Schnabel, 189.

177 Polhill, 97–98.

178 Schnabel, 193. One must remember that, because of the destruction of the Northern Kingdom of Israel and then the exile of Judah, there were Jews scattered throughout the region. Those who were still faithful to YHWH would have came at various times for the religious holidays.

179 Schnabel, 202-203.

180 Polhill, 109.

181 Seth D. Postell, "Psalm 16: The Resurrected Messiah," in *The Moody Handbook of Messianic Prophecy: Studies and Expositions of the Messiah in the Old Testament*, ed. Michael Rydelnik and Edwin Blum (Chicago, IL: Moody Publishers, 2019), 513.

182 Michael A. Rydelnik, "Psalm 110: The Messiah as Eternal King Priest," in *The Moody Handbook of Messianic Prophecy: Studies and Expositions of the Messiah in the Old Testament*, ed. Michael Rydelnik and Edwin Blum (Chicago, IL: Moody Publishers, 2019), 687.

183 F.F. Bruce, *Acts*, The New International Commentary On the New Testament (Grand Rapids: Eerdmans, 1988), 68.

184 Schnabel, 272-273.

185 Polhill, 116.

186 Grudem, 634.

187 There is much scholarly debate on whether Jude is quoting the historical Enoch, the book of 1 Enoch, or both.

188 Craig S. Keener, *Revelation*, The NIV Application Commentary (Grand Rapids, MI: Zondervan Publishing House, 1999), 453.

189 Robert H. Mounce, *The Book of Revelation*, The New International Commentary on the New Testament (Grand Rapids, MI: Wm. B. Eerdmans Publishing Co., 1997), 351. Indeed, some have this idea that the God of the Old Testament was vengeful, while Jesus in the New Testament is only loving. In reality, both YHWH in the Old Testament and Jesus in the New Testament have a strong mixture of patience, love, and judgment.

190 Buist M. Fanning, *Revelation*, Zondervan Exegetical Commentary on the New Testament (Grand Rapids: Zondervan, 2020), 188.

191 Ed Hindson, *Revelation: Unlocking the Future*, Twenty-First Century Biblical Commentary Series (Chattanooga: AMG Publishers, 2002), 81.

192 Hindson, 195.

193 Robert L. Thomas, *Revelation*, Wycliffe Exegetical Commentary (Chicago: Moody Publishers, 1992), 1475. If one has ever seen the show *I Love Lucy*, there is a famous scene of Lucy in a winepress getting grape juice all over her clothes in a similar manner.

194 Alan F. Johnson, *Revelation*, The Expositor's Bible Commentary (Grand Rapids: Zondervan, 2006), loc. 6270.

195 Mounce, 355.

196 Charles R. Swindoll, *Insights on Revelation*, Swindoll's Living Insights New Testament Commentary Book (Caroll Stream: Tyndale House Publishers, 2014), 425.

197 Thomas, 1485.

198 Timothy J. Demy, "Lake of Fire," ed. Ed Hindson, Mark Hitchcock, and Tim LaHaye, *The Harvest Handbook of Bible Prophecy* (Eugene, OR: Harvest House Publishers, 2020), 212.

www.ingramcontent.com/pod-product-compliance
Lightning Source LLC
Chambersburg PA
CBHW050647160426
43194CB00010B/1838